KAMLOOPA

LOVE LETTERS TO KAMLOOPA

Kamloopa,
Thank you for voicing the thoughts and feelings I could never convey on my own. You have embodied and represented us all: every facet, and every strand of our interlacing, complicatedly beautiful, individual beadwork ... And as these three powerful Indigenous women go on their journeys of self-discovery and reclamation, I am moved to embrace my own journey. Like Kilawna, Mikaya, and Edith, I grew up removed from my Indigenous heritage. I do not know how to introduce myself in my Ancestors' language, and I do not have an Elder to teach me the stories and traditions of my people. But I yearn for that knowledge. Every day. I am starting to reclaim the lost parts of my heritage ... *Kamloopa,* you made me laugh. You made me cry. You made me laugh, and laugh again. *Wela'lin* & *merci.*

—MEREWYN COMEAU, ACADIENNE-MÉTISSE

Dear *Kamloopa,*
Ĩsniyés! Thank you for inviting and welcoming me to bear witness to your ceremony. I felt empowered by these beautiful, strong, and resilient women. I want to give thanks to all the Matriarchs that took part in making ceremony happen, to the beautiful grandmothers that were there to bear witness, our strong, resilient Indigenous women that helped carry the ceremony: we hold the fire together! ... *Dohã pina maač*, with love, warmth, and many blessings!

—DARYLINA POWDERFACE, NAKODA SIOUX AND BLACKFOOT

Kamloopa is a next-gen *Smoke Signals.* The Fire Carriers – Indian Friend Number 1, Kilawna, and Mikaya – all offer up some of the most genuine portrayals of what it means to be an Indigenous femme: the struggles of institutionalized colonial studies of Indigenous and settler ideologies, and how little they help; the desperation, torment, and desire for connection; the bits and pieces we bring together to find that connection and the bonds we make along the way. *Kamloopa* walks the razor's edge between the dead serious and the deadly humorous. This ceremony does not hold back ... This show is FIRE.

—RAVEN JOHN, TWO-SPIRIT TRICKSTER

From Vancouverplays.com, solicited from Indigenous womxn in lieu of critical reviews.

KAMLOOPA

AN INDIGENOUS MATRIARCH STORY

PLAY BY KIM SENKLIP HARVEY

with
the Fire Company:

Cris Derksen
Yolanda Bonnell
Daniela Masellis
Lindsay Lachance
Jessica Schacht
Michelle Chabassol
Samantha Brown
Emily Soussana
Madison Henry
Kaitlyn Yott
Samantha McCue

Talonbooks

Talonbooks
9259 Shaughnessy Street, Vancouver, British Columbia, Canada v6p 6r4
talonbooks.com

Talonbooks is located on xʷməθkʷəy̓əm, Sḵwx̱wú7mesh, and səlilwətaʔɬ Lands.

Fourth printing: 2023

Typeset in Minion
Printed and bound in Canada on 100% post-consumer recycled paper

Cover and interior design by andrea bennett, cover illustrations by Karlene Harvey

Talonbooks acknowledges the financial support of the Canada Council for the Arts, the Government of Canada through the Canada Book Fund, and the Province of British Columbia through the British Columbia Arts Council and the Book Publishing Tax Credit.

Rights to produce *Kamloopa: An Indigenous Matriarch Story*, in whole or in part, in any medium by any group, amateur or professional, are retained by the author. Interested persons are requested to contact Talonbooks, 9259 Shaughnessy Street, Vancouver, British Columbia v6p 6r4; telephone: 604-444-4889; email: info@ talonbooks.com.

LIBRARY AND ARCHIVES CANADA CATALOGUING IN PUBLICATION

Title: Kamloopa : an Indigenous matriarch story / by Kim Senklip Harvey with the Fire Company (Cris Derksen, Yolanda Bonnell, Daniela Masellis, Lindsay Lachance, Jessica Schacht, Michelle Chabassol, Samantha Brown, Emily Soussana, Madison Henry, Kaitlyn Yott, and Samantha McCue) with a foreword by Lindsay Lachance. And Fire zine! A Kamloopa study buddy / by Miki Wolf.
Other titles: Fire zine!
Names: Senklip Harvey, Kim, author. | Lachance, Lindsay, writer of foreword. | container of (work): Wolf, Miki. Fire zine.
Description: A play.
Identifiers: Canadiana 20190170417 | ISBN 9781772012422 (SOFTCOVER)
Classification: LCC PS8637.E54 K36 2019 | DDC C812/.6—dc23

Kamloopa: An Indigenous Matriarch Story

FOREWORD

Making Offers and Resonating
Our Ancestors' Dreams

by Lindsay Lachance

I'm floating. In the river. The river of my homelands. I inhale and acknowledge the Ancestors standing tall as birch trees, soaring strong as birds, and running fast as the four-legged. I'm suspended in the love of the natural world, feeling held as the fog floats in around me. This is a gift.

Making offers and giving gifts creates a true sense of reciprocity and helps me to be in relationship with what has been shared, learned, or presented. In writing this, I'm reminded of the gifts exchanged during the building and performing of *Kamloopa: An Indigenous Matriarch Story* and would like to take this opportunity to give thanks to this process and to articulate some of the transformational moments that I now carry with me.

As a dramaturge I have been gifted the privilege of reading the stories and of being in studio with various Indigenous theatre artists. After reading a draft of Kim Senklip Harvey's *Kamloopa*, I wondered how a dramaturgical process could be developed that acknowledges and focuses on the spiritual and matriarchal relationships created in her play text. I have been developing and working with what I call *Relational Indigenous Dramaturgies*. This is an attempt to articulate the various processes I'm involved in as important moments for thinking through the very political iterations of Indigenous people gathering to practise theatre in spite of the historical exclusion of Indigenous Voices, practices, and criticism from the Canadian theatrical canon. *Relational Indigenous Dramaturgies* are self-affirming practices that encourage us, as Indigenous people, to look to our own laws, practices, governance systems, and world views to create alternative ways to make our art.

While working on *Kamloopa* we participated in the Banff Centre's 2018 Playwrights Lab. Here we transformed our studio into a Women's Lodge and invited Playwrights Lab participants, Indigenous relations –

also at the Banff Centre at that time – and other guests into the Lodge. We wanted to offer a space where we felt safe to be ourselves and to invite others, including our Ancestors, our homelands, and our familial teachings, into the process. One of the guiding principles that supported the creation of *Kamloopa* was navigating how we could bring our whole selves into the process, into the room, while we worked, refusing the typical theatre training of "Leave yourself at the door." We were visited by deer, elk, birds, and bursts of wind that encouraged us that we were on the right path.

A lot of what I experience in these artistic collaborations occurs in my body and in relationship with all those presenced in the room. *Kamloopa* held a space where Indigenous practitioners presenced themselves (their homelands, languages, teachings, Creation stories, and other intangible cultural realities) in the room while we worked. I interpret these and other artistic interventions as refusals of working purely within mainstream theatre structures as we deliberately turned inwards to find the beauty, joy, and love of what our *Kamloopa* community brought to the artistic process.

A gift that Kim offered was a genuine sense of love and compassion. As you will see in Miki Wolf's "FIRE ZINE! A *Kamloopa* Study Buddy," included at the end of this book, the rehearsal process was filled with daily smudges, opening and closing circles, a wellness table, and other community-centred resources to support all of the women in the process. These offers to build and nourish relationships among a group of women-identifying theatre artists created spaces where transformation could occur.

I felt gifts being offered and transformations occurring throughout the creative process, but also throughout the performances. During a talkback after one performance at The Cultch in Vancouver, a young Indigenous woman from the audience spoke about how she had never seen herself reflected onstage or in mainstream media. She shared a similar mixed cultural ancestry as one of the Fire Holders performing in the show, and shared that for the first time she had felt seen. This is a gift. Setting out to write *Kamloopa*, Kim wanted to create a world where Indigenous women could laugh, dance, and be proud of who they are. This mandate was to counter the ongoing misrepresentations of Indigenous women in historical and contemporary media. Bearing witness to this woman's response at that talkback showed us that these joyful and truthful representations of contemporary urban Indigeneity successfully touched and transformed someone's life. She then gave a gift of jewellery, right off her wrist, to the Fire Holder that she felt connected to. A new relationship was born that night.

This publication is a gift. One that reminds its readers to be proud of who they are, to love themselves, and to enter into relationships with respect and humility. The world of *Kamloopa: An Indigenous Matriarch Story* is one that is filled with the presence and love of our Ancestors, the textures of our homelands, and the resilience of Indigenous women.

PRODUCTION HISTORY

Kamloopa was first performed between September 26 and October 6, 2018, at The Cultch's Historic Theatre in Vancouver, British Columbia, on the unceded Territories of the xʷməθkʷəy̓əm, Sḵwx̱wú7mesh, and səlilwətaʔɬ First Nations. It was co-produced by Western Canada Theatre (Tk'əmlúps / Kamloops, British Columbia), Persephone Theatre and Gordon Tootoosis Nīkānīwin Theatre (sāskwatōn / ᓵᐢᑲᑑᐣ / Saskatoon, Saskatchewan), and The Cultch, in collaboration with National Arts Centre / Centre national des Arts Indigenous Theatre (Odawa / Ottawa, Ontario) and partners Pacific Association of First Nations Women and Bill Reid Gallery of Northwest Coast Art (Vancouver, British Columbia).

The cast and crew were as follows:

MIKAYA	**SENKLIP**	**ANCESTOR:**	Kaitlyn Yott
KILAWNA	**GRIZZLY**	**ANCESTOR:**	Samantha Brown
IFN 1 (EDITH)	**RAVEN**	**ANCESTOR:**	Yolanda Bonnell

Kim Senklip Harvey, **Fire Creator** | Playwright and Director
Madison Henry, **Fire Igniter, Tender & Extinguisher** | Stage Manager
Jessica Schacht, **Fire Igniter & Tender** | Assistant Director
Michelle Chabassol, **Fire Igniter & Tender** | Apprentice Stage Manager
Lindsay Lachance, **Fire Igniter** | Dramaturge
Daniela Masellis, **Fire Igniter** | Set and Lighting Director
Samantha McCue, **Fire Igniter** | Costume Designer
Cris Derksen, **Fire Igniter** | Sound Designer and Composer
Emily Soussana, **Fire Igniter** | Projection Designer
Yolanda Bonnell, **Fire Igniter, Tender & Extinguisher**
Samantha Brown, **Fire Igniter, Tender & Extinguisher**
Kaitlyn Yott, **Fire Igniter, Tender & Extinguisher**

CHARACTERS

The three groups of characters below are each played by one actor.

MIKAYA, in her twenties, Kilawna's sister
SENKLIP, the Coyote
ANCESTOR 1

KILAWNA, in her thirties
GRIZZLY
ANCESTOR 2

INDIAN FRIEND NUMBER 1 or **IFN1** (**EDITH**), in her twenties
RAVEN
ANCESTOR 3

Presenced Beings:

The **ANCESTRAL MATRIARCHS**, eternal and living within the three women **KILAWNA**, **MIKAYA**, and **INDIAN FRIEND NUMBER 1** (**EDITH**). They are visible and present to those open to seeing them. They live within us, in the past, present, and future worlds. They are many things, including Protectors of the Spirit. They use **SHIFTERS** (**SENKLIP**, **GRIZZLY**, **RAVEN** ...) and the Elements (Air, Fire, Earth, Blood ...) to connect with us on our infinite journeys.

The **SHIFTERS**, animals who can travel between all worlds. They are able to communicate with beings in any world and inhabit those that engage with them. They are visible and present to those open to seeing them.

PLACES

The Den – sisters Kilawna and Mikaya's East Vancouver apartment.

On the Land – the British Columbia Highway 97 to Tk'əmlúps / Kamloops (British Columbia, Canada), on the sisters' Traditional Syilx Territory.

The Portal – the Powwow Arbour.

TIMES

All.

SPACES

The Multiverse.

STORYTELLER'S NOTES

There are offerings in the text, such as:

> Beat. Howls.

and:

> Beat.
>
> Heart's beat.

These came to me as I wrote this story. I gift them to you as opportunities for the actors and designers to breathe them in and interpret. They will live in your imagination, production, and spirit exactly as they should be.

By reading this story you are *presencing* Indigenous women and using blood memory. This is inextricably embedded in Indigenous Matriarchal storytelling and, therefore, the leaders creating this sacred space must be Indigenous Matriarchs.

The act of producing this story is an act of Indigenous continuance. It is a contribution to the cultural evolution of Indigenous Peoples as you will invent and create a new Indigenous ceremony.

This is an act of Indigenous invention. Be courageous, the Ancestors are watching.

NOTE ON LANGUAGE

Kamloopa: An Indigenous Matriarch Story uses lines spoken in n̓saɬxcin̓, the Indigenous language of the Syilx people. In preparation for a staging of *Kamloopa*, and out of respect and interest for the Indigenous characters in the play, we encourage you to do some research on the proper pronunciation and rhythm of the n̓saɬxcin̓ language. You might want to start with Wikipedia (try "Okanagan language") and the "nsyilxcən" page on First Voices (www.firstvoices.com/en/syilx/welcome) ... but no need to stop there! To go deeper, try contacting the Syilx/Okanagan Nation Alliance (www.syilx.org/about-us/syilx-nation/nsyilxen-language/) or meeting an Indigenous speaker of n̓saɬxcin̓.

KAMLOOPA

AN INDIGENOUS MATRIARCH STORY

THE LAND BREATHES

We see the Land forming through us.

Deep.

Beats.

The original heartbeat.

Wind is heard and then felt. The Land speaks.

This language – one that we feel – resonates.

The Land reveals everything that ever has and ever will be.

We start to hear the Ancestral Voices rise through the cacophonous spirit sounds of the Land.

The ANCESTRAL MATRIARCHS, *past, present and future, are here. Their Ancestral Voices grow and begin to evolve into a language only some will understand. They grow to a profound level and ignite the sounds of time, calling for witnesses.*

ANCESTRAL MATRIARCHS: (*speaking in* ṅsəĺxciṅ, *the mother tongue of the Syilx First Nation*) kʷú áláʔ, kʷú mínímɬtət, kʷú áláʔ. stəmtəmkílt. słáłákíx̌áʔ. kʷú skʷlk̓ʷált, i sásátíkʷ, i stk̓másq̓t, i tmix̌ʷ, i słúx̌słúx̌ncútət il təmx̌ʷláx̌tət. nyáʕíp əcmístm kɬ x̌ʷílwís klánwí. kʷú təmx̌ʷúláx̌ʷ, i snílítəntət mí kʷ cblák̓.

(*Here. Us. We are here. Daughters. Sisters. We are the mountains, the rivers, the sky, the animals, the wind, the breath of our worlds. These are the pathways connecting us to you. We are the Land, our home for you to return to, together.*)

A destructive, masculine beat.

The actions of time attempt to erase the
ANCESTRAL MATRIARCHS.

The RAVEN, *the* SENKLIP, *and the*
GRIZZLY *appear.*

EDITH, MIKAYA, *and* KILAWNA *follow and move*
in relationship with their Animals.

ANCESTRAL MATRIARCHS: (*speaking n̓səl̓xciɰ̓*) íʔlíx̌ iʔl snútíkʷ,
nyáʕíp sɬx̌ʷncútx̌.

(*Stay on the Wind River, keep breathing.*)

Hearts are beating together.

RAVEN EDITH, SENKLIP MIKAYA, *and* GRIZZLY
KILAWNA *are one. We hear their Land Song;*
it sounds like the breath and life of Mother Earth.

A suspension.

The masculine beating excavates the Animals from
the ANCESTRAL MATRIARCHS, *who are displaced*
from the Land.

RAVEN, SENKLIP, *and* GRIZZLY *get on the*
Wind River.

The ANCESTRAL MATRIARCHS *struggle to breathe.*

ANCESTRAL MATRIARCHS: lút nyáʕíp kʷú t̓ə knánáqs. kúcʔúllús
nyáʕíp i k̓lx̌áʔx̌ítət.

(*We are never alone. Our Ancestors are with us. Together*
forever.)

Somewhere between this world and the last...

... lut kʷu‿t̓ə‿x̌ast

We are not well...

IN SEARCH OF

*A two-bedroom apartment in East Vancouver,
British Columbia. The suite is modest,
complicated, white.*

*MIKAYA is on the couch and lurches into this
world. She grabs her shoulder and yelps in pain,
tries to find her human breath. She stumbles into
the kitchen and douses her face with water.*

*Her sister KILAWNA exits her room with a laundry
basket and sees MIKAYA in the kitchen, her
head drenched.*

KILAWNA: What's wrong with you?

*MIKAYA shakes her head and winces from the
pain in her shoulder.*

MIKAYA: I... I don't know.

*KILAWNA starts to grab dishcloths and towels
laying around the den.*

KILAWNA: Don't you have class?

MIKAYA: I don't want to go.

KILAWNA: You gotta grow that brain.

MIKAYA imitates her white professor.

MIKAYA: "Mikaya, would you like to share with your peers the
meaning behind Coast Salish weavings."

*MIKAYA points to one of the European art history
books from her classes that is sitting on the
coffee table.*

MIKAYA: I know more about this culture than about being an indian. It's like she assumes we all just waltzed in from a Vision Quest.

KILAWNA: They find out you're Native and everyone looks at you with these constipated faces. Like you were once a real person and then all of a sudden you're in a museum, standing behind the glass, holding a basket of corn.

KILAWNA looks at the laundry basket.

MIKAYA: Or they expect you to be able to weave, sing, and dance.

MIKAYA checks herself out using the selfie function on her phone and makes duck faces.

KILAWNA: Don't be vain.

MIKAYA: Useless, producing no result.

KILAWNA: Huh?

Beat.

Heart's beat.

MIKAYA: My skin is so light.

KILAWNA: Get a spray tan.

MIKAYA: I wish my cheeks weren't so chubby.

KILAWNA: Stop eating Cheezies.

MIKAYA: I wish I looked more...

MIKAYA manipulates her body to look "more indian," but she ends up looking like one of those wooden figures depicting Indigenous people that you find outside cigar stores.

KILAWNA: Constipated?

MIKAYA imitates Pocahontas making the "goodbye" gesture.

MIKAYA: *Wingapo.*

KILAWNA: Whatever, Pinocchio.

MIKAYA: Fuck Pinocchio. I'm Pocahontas.

Beat.

MIKAYA: Isn't life's lesson number one something like, "Knowing who you are is the key to your future"?

KILAWNA: Did you read that on a poster in your social science class?

MIKAYA: Ya, I did, that and: "You miss one hundred percent of the shots you don't take."

KILAWNA: I gotta get to work.

KILAWNA grabs her things and heads to leave.

The Wind River blows through.

MIKAYA: If they wanted to hear about the violent impacts of colonization, I could have told them. Or about the systematic dissemination of Settler supremacy, I could do that too. I guess I just...

KILAWNA: Don't let these leftist, white, liberal women professors get to you. You're fine, it's fine. This... indian thing. Just leave it alone.

MIKAYA jumps onto the couch and hits play on her laptop. It's the song "Colors of the Wind" from Disney's 1995 animated film Pocahontas. KILAWNA grabs her things and heads out the door.

MIKAYA sings the song's first verse or so, mockingly but affectionately, mistaking some of the words.

KILAWNA: Those aren't the words. Bye.

KILAWNA exits. MIKAYA starts to pant.

FIRST CONTACT

MIKAYA *plays "Colors of the Wind" from Disney's* Pocahontas *and starts to fall asleep. It transforms into the* ANCESTRAL MATRIARCHS's *Land Song.*

The Wind River flows in.

MIKAYA *hears something.*

MIKAYA: Hello? Kilawna?

She goes to investigate, but then goes back into the den and falls away from this world.

The Wind River drains.

IN THE DEN

MIKAYA is asleep, burrowed on the couch.
KILAWNA enters from her bedroom and
approaches her sister. She adjusts the blanket and
leans in lovingly.

KILAWNA: WAKE UP!

MIKAYA wakes up and, still immersed in
Pocahontas's "Colors of the Wind," blurts out:

MIKAYA: SAVAGES, SAVAGES!

KILAWNA imitates a Hollywood clichéd
"slow-talking Indian."

KILAWNA: My name is Mikaya. I currently live on this couch.
I come from the Traditional Territory of the Lazy People.
My Spirit Animal is the gopher.

Beating.

KILAWNA: It's so important, Little Sleeping Gopher, that you get
up, sleep in a real bed, live life, like the super indian you are.

MIKAYA gets up and goes to make coffee.

KILAWNA: How long is this Las Vegas residency on the couch
going to be for?

MIKAYA: I'm exhausted but I can't sleep... I close my eyes and
I'm more awake...

KILAWNA: But then you sleep all day. You've got to break
the cycle.

MIKAYA: Cycle?

KILAWNA: Yes. Tomorrow morning, set your alarm, and get up
early. That way at nighttime you're tired.

MIKAYA: Been having these weird dreams...

The faint sound of the heartbeat. The ANCESTRAL
MATRIARCHS *are coming.*

The Wind river blows through.

RAVEN *honks.*

MIKAYA *starts to go through her school papers.*

MIKAYA: How do we pronounce "Okanagan" traditionally again?

KILAWNA shrugs. MIKAYA *opens one of her
text books.*

MIKAYA: Did you know that in my three years of being at
university, I've never set foot in a library?

KILAWNA: And you're proud of this?

KILAWNA shakes her head disapprovingly.

MIKAYA: Prof Debra and I got a good thing going on. She singles
me out, pushes me to my limit of comfortability, hustles her
white-liberal agenda; I push back, and in return she gives me
white-guilt pity marks.

KILAWNA: Careful not to set the bar too high.

MIKAYA: Couldn't if I cared.

Drum. Beats.

MIKAYA: (*emphasizing the guttural quality of the word*)
"Silllxch" – we're Syilx.

KILAWNA looks at MIKAYA.

MIKAYA: Prof Debra put me on the spot the other day and I
completely flubbed it. Then this super-Indigenous woman
stood up and schooled me. She stood up in front of the whole
lecture hall and shared a story from her Nation and then
spoke in her language. Then a ray of light came through the
roof as a drum appeared in her hand and an eagle landed on

11

her shoulder and they sang a song together around a fire that just suddenly, poof, appeared.

KILAWNA: Mikaya.

MIKAYA: She turned everyone's constipated faces into these enlightened looks of ease and contentment.

Heart beats.

MIKAYA: I want to do that! I want to influence the wind with my mind, the sun with my songs, and the birds with my stories.

KILAWNA: You want to show off in front of a bunch of white people?

MIKAYA: I don't know... Do you ever feel like being Indigenous, it... it's, it's...

MIKAYA scans the surfaces of her body.

KILAWNA: I don't know what you're talking about.

MIKAYA: Don't you ever feel like a phony?

KILAWNA: I don't feel much about it.

MIKAYA: Well some of us experience emotions.

KILAWNA: Some of us experience enough emotions for the both of us.

The Wind River flows. The ANCESTRAL MATRIARCHS are calling SENKLIP.

MIKAYA: Did you hear something?

KILAWNA: No.

MIKAYA: I think I'm hearing things.

KILAWNA: What's wrong with you?

MIKAYA: I can't see what's right in front of my face.

KILAWNA: Just do your school work and stop fucking around. Being Indigenous is just being… it's just a… a punishment.

Beat. Howls.

MIKAYA: Here comes the Native hate.

KILAWNA: Whatever.

MIKAYA: Superb.

KILAWNA: Fantastic.

MIKAYA: Stupendous.

KILAWNA: Excellent.

MIKAYA: Tremendous.

KILAWNA: Take a shower.

MIKAYA: I don't need to.

MIKAYA pulls out dry shampoo from the couch and wallows in it.

MIKAYA: So fresh and so clean, so clean!

KILAWNA walks towards her room. She gives MIKAYA the middle finger without turning around.

SMOKESCREENS

MIKAYA *is standing on the couch. She's wearing a salad bowl on her head to imitate a woven cedar hat and has wrapped herself in a blanket to make it look like a Coast Salish traditional garment. The music is blaring: it's "O Siem" by Susan Aglukark (ᓱᓴ ᐊᒡᔪᒃᑲᖅ suusan agluukkaq) and Chad Irschick, sung by Aglukark.* MIKAYA *is singing along, pretending to be a dancer. She's created a hybrid of Indigenous-looking gestures inspired by what she's seen on* TV *and her very little understanding of the Indigenous dances she's seen in and around Vancouver – the Haida button-blanket dance, for example.*

MIKAYA *moves all around the apartment, dancing and singing, picking up items and pretending to bless them. She gains confidence and boldness as the song progresses. She picks up a broom and uses it as microphone, then as a talking stick.*

She starts speaking a made-up Indigenous language, inspired by some of the guttural sounds found in Coast Salish languages like hǝṅq̓ǝmiṅǝṁ and Sḵwx̱wú7mesh.

MIKAYA: *How, slottlen. Meeskootla, schleka'naw… Jesus, I sound Czech.*

She takes the bowl off her head and throws it across the room.

RAVEN *honks.*

MIKAYA *goes to her room, angry.*

KILAWNA enters the front door and notices how messy the den is.

Growl.

KILAWNA: Mikaya.

Growling.

KILAWNA: Mikaya!

MIKAYA starts blaring music from her bedroom. KILAWNA, frustrated, starts to clean up the apartment. MIKAYA enters the den dressed up for a night out on the town. She goes into the kitchen and cracks open a cider.

KILAWNA: It's a Tuesday.

MIKAYA chugs the entire cider and burps.

Howls.

MIKAYA: It's turn-it-up fuckin' Tuesday, you know?

MIKAYA walks to the fridge and opens a bottle of wine, pours a glass, and takes some healthy sips.

KILAWNA: Pour me a glass.

MIKAYA races and slides into the kitchen to pour KILAWNA an even healthier glass of wine.

KILAWNA: Turn-it-up Tuesdays.

MIKAYA: Yeah Siiiiis!

KILAWNA takes a sip of wine and smiles. MIKAYA finishes her wine. She finds some old booze in a cupboard and pours it into shot glasses.

KILAWNA: (*excited*) Ahhh hah! Yes!

MIKAYA: (*imitating a cowgirl on a horse*) YEA, YEA, YEA, YEA!

MIKAYA saunters like a spur-wearing dueller. KILAWNA whistles the stereotypical Spaghetti Western theme, as in the two-note flute motif and "wah-wah-wah" incantations of Ennio Morricone's main theme for Sergio Leone's 1966 film The Good, the Bad and the Ugly.

KILAWNA: *Wah, wah, waaaaah...*

MIKAYA: *Wah, wah, waaaaah...*

BOTH: *Wah, wah wah waaaaaaaah... Wah, wah waaaaaaah.*

They drink the shots, then both dramatically fall to the floor.

MIKAYA: I've been shot!

MIKAYA grabs her heart.

MIKAYA: (*quoting a line from the 1998 movie* Smoke Signals *by Chris Eyre*) "Hey Victor!"

KILAWNA: (*same*) "Why'd your Dad leave?"

KILAWNA starts to walk to her room and begins to take off her work clothes in the process.

MIKAYA: (*quoting approximately*) "When Indians leave, they don't come back – like in *The Last of the Mohicans*..."

Beat.

MIKAYA: (*pestering KILAWNA for attention*) Hey! Hey! Hey!

MIKAYA impersonates Daniel Day Lewis as Hawkeye (a.k.a Nathaniel Poe and La Longue Carabine) in Michael Mann's 1992 film The Last of the Mohicans.

MIKAYA: "No! You stay alive! If they *don't* kill you, they'll take you north, up to the Huron Land. You're strong! You survive! You stay alive! I *will* find you!!!"

MIKAYA stops her impersonation and starts teasing her sister.

MIKAYA: Hey! Hey! Hey! Hey, Kilawna! Hey, Kilawna!!!

KILAWNA: (*from the bedroom*) Hey yourself, you fucking horse.

MIKAYA: You hear that raven flying around the 'hood lately?

KILAWNA emerges from her bedroom looking like a ninety-year-old woman, wearing a housecoat, no bra, and a terrifying face mask.

MIKAYA: Not allowed.

KILAWNA: This is my regime.

MIKAYA: Well you look like a vagine.

KILAWNA: Pardon me?

MIKAYA: We're going out tonight!

KILAWNA: I am not.

MIKAYA: We are.

KILAWNA: I have an early-morning meeting tomorrow and it's already late.

MIKAYA: (*looking at her watch*) It's 6:30 p.m.

KILAWNA: Jesus Christ, that's it?

MIKAYA pulls out a makeup bag from the couch.

KILAWNA: What's that?

MIKAYA: War paint.

SENKLIP starts to lure GRIZZLY.

KILAWNA: So get this. Today this HR lady was like, "Yo, you're an Indian, you get massages and extra stuff."

MIKAYA: What?

KILAWNA: Ya, she just yelled it out.

MIKAYA: Like, in your office?

KILAWNA: In the middle of the staff meeting.

MIKAYA: You have got to be kidding me!?

KILAWNA: Nope.

MIKAYA: Was her name Debra?

KILAWNA: Stephanie.

MIKAYA: Stephanie sounds like a total moron.

KILAWNA: (*imitating Stephanie*) "Noooooo, I'm great. I hire the best people. I just read an article about Reconciliation and now I feel *allll* better."

    KILAWNA finishes her wine.

MIKAYA: We don't get "extra" stuff, we get a piss-poor excuse of reparations from the federal government and the worst health coverage in the history of Canada.

KILAWNA: Yes. Two massages in exchange for ten trillion hectares of land – seems fair.

MIKAYA: I've laid your clothes out on your bed.

KILAWNA: Thank you.

MIKAYA: I think this Stephanie sounds like a white supremacist.

KILAWNA: (*aghast*) Uhhhh... I don't think so.

    KILAWNA goes to change.

MIKAYA: (*lecturing*) We're inundated by systems created by imperialism, upheld by Settlers, designed by the state with the desire to kill us. Like, from day one they oppressed systems to take advantage of us. Look at Hudson's Bay, for example.

KILAWNA: I love the Bay.

MIKAYA: The Canadian government denies their continued involvement in the genocide of Indigenous Peoples and sells us this narrative that Canadians are "nice."

KILAWNA: I wonder what Bay Days were like when they first opened.

MIKAYA: And we're left to look like the savages calling murder and guilt on the Settlers. Like, they used chemical warfare by hiding smallpox in our blankets!

KILAWNA: That gives a whole new meaning to the phrase "scratch and save."

MIKAYA: One good thing about the KKK recently rearing their disgusting faces is that people can no longer deny the presence of white supremacy. It's everywhere, they are everywhere. They're in your staff meetings, lecture halls, courtrooms...

KILAWNA: They are serving your drinks, telling you about your union benefits, they are your bosses, soccer moms, art enthusiasts, they are filling out your prescription medications...

KILAWNA: (*imitating a pharmacist in a drugstore on a PA system*) "Indian (*cough, cough*), Indian, we have your medication ready, Indian. I'm looking for an Indian in the store. We have your government-paid-for, *free* medication. Please ensure you bring out your identification to ensure we know you're a freeloading Indian. Indian, Indian, we're paging an Indian..."

> *KILAWNA starts to sing the second verse of "Feed the Birds" from the 1964 Disney movie Mary Poppins.*

KILAWNA: It's like the pharmacists, it's like everyone, every fucking neo-libertarian becomes Julie fucking Andrews and they treat us like the goddamn pigeons.

MIKAYA *pretends to be something in between a pigeon and an impoverished person, grabbing and eating the fake food/medicine* KILAWNA *is throwing around the apartment. She joins in singing "Tuppence, tuppence, tuppence a bag." The music of "Feed the Birds" comes in loud and we see* SENKLIP *and* GRIZZLY *entwined with* MIKAYA *and* KILAWNA. *The feral beings take shots, dance, and destroy the apartment.* MIKAYA *punches a hole in the wall.* KILAWNA *laughs and sticks her head in it. The song morphs into a remix of Pocahontas's "Savages" and A Tribe Called Red's "Sila," featuring Tanya Tagaq. They have gone to a place beyond human forms. They grab their bags and head out the door.*

Growls. Snarls.

RAVEN *flies after them.*

SISTERS

The next morning. KILAWNA *is on the couch. She sits up and we see that her makeup is smeared across her face. She is wearing an Indigenous headband made out of a garbage bag.*

KILAWNA: My brain is coming out of my butthole.

She takes a swig out of the water bottle on the table. It's some kind of alcohol they syphoned. She spits it out.

KILAWNA: What the fuck is that?!

MIKAYA *exits from* KILAWNA'*s room on all fours.*

KILAWNA: What are you doing?

MIKAYA *keeps crawling towards the couch and slowly starts to get up.*

MIKAYA: Nope, nope, noooooope, oh noooo.

She gets back down on all fours, crawls to the couch, and curls up next to KILAWNA.

KILAWNA: What happened?

MIKAYA: That was so much fun! We should do that more.

KILAWNA: No, like, I actually don't remember.

MIKAYA: Oh shit, really?

KILAWNA: This is worse than the time I woke up in bed naked with a poutine next to me. Can I please get a recap?

MIKAYA: Ya.

MIKAYA *reaches for the same water bottle*
KILAWNA *previously drank out of and*
takes a swig.

KILAWNA: Wait!!!

MIKAYA *swallows and thinks for a second.*

MIKAYA: Gin and tonic.

KILAWNA: So what happened last night?

MIKAYA: Well, we started here and you put on a *Golden Girls* outfit and looked really baaaad –

KILAWNA: I remember that part.

MIKAYA: Good, because you need to stop dressing like that.

KILAWNA: Go on.

MIKAYA: Then we went to Tubby's.

KILAWNA *is disgusted at the name and at the fact that she ended up at this place.*

KILAWNA: And what, pray tell, is Tubby's?

MIKAYA: It's Tub Tub's.

KILAWNA: Saying it twice doesn't help me understand

MIKAYA: Tuberon's... Tuuuuuubs... Tub a Bub... Tub Flub... Tubby, Tubby, Flubby Tubby.

KILAWNA: What happened at Tubby's?!

MIKAYA: Drawing a blank.

KILAWNA: You said you remembered!

MIKAYA: (*imitating an old lady*) I'm an old woman losing my memory. Now where did I put my teeth?

KILAWNA: This isn't funny. What we did was super dangerous and irresponsible.

KILAWNA goes into the bathroom and takes a shower.

MIKAYA: Oh relax.

MIKAYA shakes her head and is surprised that she still can't remember. She perks up and remembers.

MIKAYA: PHONES! Check the phones!!!

KILAWNA: (*from the shower*) What?!

MIKAYA sees her purse under the kitchen table and lunges for it. She dumps the contents out on the table: bouncy balls, a fan, a dozen lipsticks, condoms, floss, and one flip-flop fall out, but no phone.

MIKAYA: Goddammit!

MIKAYA looks around and spots KILAWNA's purse on the table. She jumps over the couch and dials her own number. Her phone rings: it's coming from the fridge. She opens the salad spinner and there it is.

She yells to KILAWNA.

MIKAYA: Nothing on Facebook. Can't see anything on Insta. Weird, neither of us did any Snaps. Twitter: I didn't send any tweets. *You* did, though!

KILAWNA: (*from the bathroom*) What?

MIKAYA: Yep.

KILAWNA: What does it say?

MIKAYA: "@TheRealAdamBeach, why did they give you such a terrible wig @ the end of *Smoke Signals*? #JohnWaynesTeeth #Kocoum #IndianFriendNumber1"

KILAWNA exits from the bathroom in a robe.

KILAWNA: Okay, well I guess it could be worse. I should delete it though.

MIKAYA: NO! He could respond. It's a valid question. The people need answers: that wig *was* terrible.

KILAWNA: I'm going to be late for work.

MIKAYA: Reeeelaaaax, you're never late.

KILAWNA: I hate that stupid "Indian time" shit.

MIKAYA: Being late every once in a while doesn't make you a part of some racist stereotype.

KILAWNA: Tell that to Stephanie. And last night was a mistake. We can't be acting like a bunch of drunk indians. You know what other people think when they see us out like that?

MIKAYA: That we're drunk Mexicans?

KILAWNA: No! They see a couple of good-for-nothing indian women. When we go out, we are not just representing us, we're representing an entire race of people!

MIKAYA: No pressure.

KILAWNA: People judge us for who we are and what we do.

MIKAYA: When Debra and Stephanie go out, it's just two people going out. Why are we drunks when we do it? Going out and having fun and going dancing doesn't make us a couple of good-for-nothing drunk indians.

KILAWNA walks towards her bedroom.

Beat.

KILAWNA: I'm going to be late for work.

MIKAYA blinks and slowly goes to sit on the couch.

MIKAYA: (*trying to remember*) Tubby's and then...

KILAWNA: Shit. I can't find my keys or phone.

KILAWNA finds her phone on the coffee table and briefly looks at it.

KILAWNA: Indian Friend Number 1... whatever. Where are my keys?

KILAWNA starts searching around the apartment which is already quite the disaster.

KILAWNA: Please, help me.

MIKAYA: Okay, okay, okay.

MIKAYA attempts to get up and starts crawling around. She empties a bag of cereal.

KILAWNA: It's not cereal time, it's help-me-find-my-phone time.

MIKAYA: I *am* helping you.

KILAWNA starts searching around more frantically and muttering under her breath.

KILAWNA: Where could they be...

KILAWNA now sees MIKAYA going through the bowls, dishtowels, and the mess of the den.

KILAWNA: Mikaya, my keys are not in the fucking dish towels.

MIKAYA: My phone was in the salad spinner, so who knows where your keys are!

KILAWNA holds her ground.

KILAWNA: This is why I don't like doing shit like last night.

KILAWNA trips over some clothes that are on the ground.

MIKAYA: Hey! That's my coat.

MIKAYA throws a dish towel in her direction.

KILAWNA: It's always a fucking mess, your shit is everywhere. I can't find anything ever.

MIKAYA: *Your* shit is everywhere, none of this shit is even mine. You won't even let me choose the fucking calendar.

> *KILAWNA stomps over to the calendar on the wall and comes to full standing.*

KILAWNA: Because when you did choose the calendar you got a Tonto and Lone Ranger one!!!

MIKAYA: I was being ironic!

KILAWNA: Where are my fucking keys?!!

> *INDIAN FRIEND NUMBER 1 (IFN1) emerges from MIKAYA's bedroom wearing a custom-made housecoat.*

IFN1: Here they are.

> *IFN1 tosses KILAWNA's keys, which go flying into the wall. IFN1 hops into the bathroom.*

IFN1: *OOOOOOO SIEM*, Friends!

> *IFN1 raises her right hand in a fist and shuts the door.*

> *MIKAYA's jaw drops and KILAWNA's eyes nearly pop out of her head. We hear a giant fart coming from the bathroom.*

IFN1: (*offstage*) Excuse me.

> *We hear the toilet flush, some gargling, some aerosol-can noise, drawers opening and closing, a smaller fart, more aerosol-can noise ... The door opens. IFN1 goes back into MIKAYA's room and gives MIKAYA a butt slap as she journeys through.*

KILAWNA: Who the fuck is that?

> *MIKAYA shrugs and knocks on the bedroom door.*

KILAWNA: Why are you knocking?

MIKAYA: I don't know.

IFN1 emerges and smiles at both of them. She walks towards the kitchen, grabs some juice from the fridge, and starts to drink it from the carton.

IFN1: You girls are wiiiiiiiild.

MIKAYA has a light-bulb moment.

MIKAYA: Kilawna! Your phone! Indian Friend Number 1.

IFN1: That's me!

KILAWNA grabs her phone and starts reading out loud the text messages from the most recent senders.

KILAWNA: "Hey, Victor"… "Where the Hawkins at?"… "Bring hot dogs"… "Shot shot shots"… "Good job on riding the bull." Mikaya, can you deal with this?!

MIKAYA: (*to IFN1*) Are you going to rob us?

IFN1: Nope.

To KILAWNA.

MIKAYA: I got this.

KILAWNA is exasperated and late. She picks up her keys and looks back into the kitchen to IFN1. IFN1 looks right back at her and makes a cheers motion with the juice jug. KILAWNA stares back, and we hear another fart.

MIKAYA: That one was me.

KILAWNA shakes her head and exits out the front door.

IFN1 starts wandering around the apartment holding her juice, taking sips. MIKAYA sits on the couch, taking IFN1 in.

IFN1: What are we up for today?

MIKAYA: I was just, uh...

IFN1 is confused by MIKAYA's hesitation.

IFN1: You go to school?

MIKAYA nods.

IFN1: That's cool, that's cool. What are you studying at school?

MIKAYA: Haven't declared a major yet. Maybe English. I like Native studies but it just seems too ironic. Probs just going to fuck it all up anyways.

IFN1: You shouldn't do that.

Off.

Beat.

MIKAYA: What are you doing today?

IFN1: Well we planned a whole list of things to accomplish last night.

MIKAYA: I'm having a bit of a hard time remembering what exactly happened last night.

She pants.

IFN1: All good my sister, all good.

IFN1 perches.

IFN1: Lesson number one: You have got to stop dismissing yourself. All last night you just keep shutting yourself down. Putting yourself down is the royal road to depression.

MIKAYA: I... I'm not...

IFN1: (*mimicking*) I... I... I... A guy came up to you last night and said you had nice hair, and your response was, "I look like a troll doll."

MIKAYA *gently pats her hair.*

IFN1: Then at the indian bar, a hot Kocoum started talking about his dope-ass drum group and you started going on a rant about how the Settlers have robbed us of everything and how we're all doomed, like some kind of *Last of the Mohicans* shit.

MIKAYA: Well we ar–

IFN1: Last night you enrolled in my school of How to Become a Real Indian, and if I'm going to teach you, you've got to stop putting yourself down. Lesson number one: Believe in the brown.

Ancestral.

Calls.

IFN1: You said that you didn't know any cultural things. That you didn't have a single indian friend. So I'm it, I'm your Indian Friend Number 1.

IFN1 gives the slightly terrified MIKAYA a big grin.
MIKAYA pants and barks.

IFN1: You okay?

MIKAYA: Yeah, yes. For sure, please.

IFN1: Excellent. Class is in session and the indian teachings are out there!

IFN1: (*pointing to the door*) Let's go find them.

MIKAYA: Now?

IFN1: Yeah!

MIKAYA: (*suddenly enthusiastic*) Yes!!

IFN1 and MIKAYA run out of the apartment. They re-enter, realizing IFN1 is not wearing any clothes and neither of them have shoes on. They go into MIKAYA's room to get dressed.

DEN MATES

Same day. KILAWNA *enters the apartment,*
exhausted and slightly disheveled. The apartment
is a mess – still. She lumbers around, tidying the
den, and begins to assemble some food. MIKAYA
enters the apartment.

MIKAYA: Hello. I'm home.

KILAWNA goes into her room and shuts the door to
take a phone call.

MIKAYA: Who ya talking to?

Silence.

MIKAYA: Kilawna.

Barks.

MIKAYA: I hung out with that woman we found in our apartment
earlier.

Wind.

MIKAYA: I was able to put last night's events together.

KILAWNA re-enters the den.

KILAWNA: And?

MIKAYA: After Tubby's, we went to play bingo, and then we went
to the indian bar.

KILAWNA hangs her head in shame.

MIKAYA: Ya, we met her at Tubs, and then I told her how much I
wanted to be a... how much we... how it's important that we
know what it really means to be Indigenous, and she said she
would help.

Bark.

MIKAYA: Lots of indians at the bingo hall.

KILAWNA: That's unfortunate.

Bark.

MIKAYA: It was pretty cool, Sis. We got to hang out with real indians.

KILAWNA: Did someone win some money?

MIKAYA: Yes! On pull tabs.

KILAWNA: Just when I thought we couldn't fulfill any more stereotypes.

MIKAYA: It was awesome.

KILAWNA: Did you go to school today?

MIKAYA: Wellllll...

KILAWNA: (*reproachfully*) Mikaya...

Beat.

MIKAYA: Indian Friend Number 1 told me that we learn our culture outside.

KILAWNA: What, so now she's Grandmother Willow?

MIKAYA: Look I just learn different, like a monastery.

KILAWNA: Montessori.

MIKAYA: Sure.

IFN1 kicks open the door. She's dressed like a stereotypical Medicine Woman and a superhero.

IFN1: (*greeting* KILAWNA *and* MIKAYA *in* həṅ̓q̓əmiṅ̓əṁ) HÁY ČX^w Q̓Ə, BITCHES! Teachers on campus! BANG, BANG!

IFN1 tosses a stack of books over to the coffee table in the middle of the room. The impact breaks two

*of the table's legs and it collapses. They all stand in
disbelief for a second.*

IFN1: Must've already been busted. Hey, Ki Ki, looking good
sister, as per use, as per use. Mik, get over here, teacher's
gotta teach.

KILAWNA: What?

IFN1: Mikaya's enrolled in my school of How to Become a Real
Indian.

MIKAYA: (*to* KILAWNA) Personal development.

*MIKAYA smiles, heads towards the coffee table, and
attempts to fix it.*

IFN1: Let's start by seeing what you already know.

MIKAYA nods.

IFN1: What is an indian's favourite food?

MIKAYA: Bannock.

IFN1: Wrong!

MIKAYA: Shit, I mean: salmon.

*KILAWNA rolls her eyes and keeps eating
her dinner.*

IFN1: Who represents our wants and needs jurisdictionally?

MIKAYA: Uhhh… Even though 70 percent of Indigenous Peoples
live off reserve, we have no official legislative representation at
the provincial and federal levels.

IFN1: Who are our unofficial Nation-to-Nation Ambassadors?

MIKAYA: The Assembly of First Nations.

IFN1: People think that, but the real control lies elsewhere. In the
'90s it was held by the indian portion of the cast of *North
of 60* and *Dances with Wolves*. But over the past ten years a

grassroots movement has occurred with the rise of hip hop and electronic music. So our current reps are...

MIKAYA and IFN1: A TRIBE CALLED RED!!!

IFN1 hits play on the laptop that's sitting on the broken coffee table and out comes A Tribe Called Red's "Sisters," featuring Northern Voice. IFN1 starts doing her best prairie chicken dance – but looks more like a manic monkey. MIKAYA joins in, equally terrible but committed. The whole episode ends with IFN1 pulling an air horn out of her pants and blasting it. KILAWNA stands there unimpressed.

IFN1: What are the four Teachings of the Cultural Medicine Wheel to let Settlers know that we're indians?

MIKAYA: Number one: Our hair – must be kept long and parted in the centre.

MIKAYA quickly adjusts her hair and parts it in the centre. IFN1 gives háy čxʷ q̓əs in approval.

IFN1: Number two?

MIKAYA: Number two: Wear a tasteful amount of Native jewellery. Historically, silver and turquoise were predominantly the most effective indicators, as well as bone chokers, which became a staple in our wardrobes for those "I need you to know that I'm an indian" moments.

IFN1: And now?

MIKAYA: *(trying to think of the answer)* And now... now...

IFN1: And now the popular choice is Coast Salish silver and gold jewellery – *(showing off her accessories)* pendants! Necklaces! Bracelets! Ringgggs!

MIKAYA: And contemporary T-shirts and apparel that tastefully communicate our indian identities.

IFN1: And number three?

MIKAYA: Number three: We must introduce ourselves in our mother tongues – that is the ultimate act of decolonization. We must learn to introduce ourselves in our Indigenous languages.

IFN1: And what do we do if we don't have access to a sacred language speaker?

MIKAYA: We piece together something from the internet and hope for the best. Settlers will never know.

IFN1: Exactly!

IFN1 says something she may have heard in hǝṅ̓q̓ǝmiṅ̓ǝm̓, although uncomprehendingly.

MIKAYA: What did you say?

IFN1: Who knows?!!

MIKAYA: Right, okay. And we can also, with the utmost respect, adopt small hand gestures of the peoples whose Territory we reside on. For example, "háy čxʷ q̓ǝ" is the hǝṅ̓q̓ǝmiṅ̓ǝm̓ expression for "Welcome" and "Thank you." And their hand gesture is this.

MIKAYA raises her arms up, elbows bent and palms facing in, and moves them right to left repeatedly in a very exaggerated way. She "welcomes" the whole apartment. When she gets to KILAWNA, she does it with a big closed-mouth smile. KILAWNA shakes her head.

IFN1: And number four?

MIKAYA: Ummm...

IFN1: Number four: When all else fails, get annnngryyyy! Call them a Settler! And use the word "colonialism"...

MIKAYA *joins in and echoes* IFN1*'s teachings with enthusiasm.*

IFN1: ... and "cultural genocide" a lot. Implore a heavy use of "my people" and mention your Ancestors as much as you caaaan!!!

Without a beat, IFN1 *and* MIKAYA *high-five and "háy čxʷ q̓ə" one another.* KILAWNA *is reading some of the handbills on the table.*

KILAWNA: What is this?

IFN1: Oooo, Silent Bear growls.

IFN1 *and* MIKAYA *walk towards the bear, getting dangerously close.*

IFN1 and MIKAYA: (*in alien-like unison*) We went to the Friendship Centre.

KILAWNA: I'm scared to go in there.

IFN1: That's what Mik said!

MIKAYA: Well I was only brave enough to do one lap of the gym, but it was awesome. It smelled like all these different spices and crafts and baked goods and had all these old women smiling.

IFN1: (*disappointed*) We went to the Aboriginal Friendship Centre, not some podunk Christmas craft fair. You weren't smelling "spices": that was sweetgrass and sage – our medicines! Those were not baked goods: they were deep and delicious bannock and jam. And those smiling women were our Elders – Red-Scarf wearing, colonization-surviving, knowledge-bearing, smoked-salmon WARRIORS!

MIKAYA: Woooo, yeahhhh!!! (*raising her arms into the air*) háy čxʷ q̓ə!

IFN1 *hops down.*

IFN1: Exactly.

She takes a seat at the table.

IFN1: We're going to the Friendship Centre for West Coast Night.

MIKAYA: That's where they dance – POWWOW.

KILAWNA: We've never been to a Powwow.

IFN1 does a twerk and sticks her tongue out.

IFN1: Just for clarification – I'm not trained in traditional indian Powwow dance – I'm self-taught.

KILAWNA: You don't say.

IFN1: Nobody said being a cultural warrior woman would be easy. I didn't have anyone teaching me this shit either. I find the internet to be most useful.

IFN1 types on a laptop sitting on the table.

IFN1: Sites like this.

Native American flute music starts playing. It's thick: long flute notes, howls, shakers, and cries.

MIKAYA: (*reading a line on the laptop's screen*) "Magical Folklore of the Red Indian Spiritual Skins."

MIKAYA starts scrolling the site.

MIKAYA: Hmmm, interesting...

KILAWNA shakes her head.

IFN1: (*reading*) "It is said that the American Indian Peoples are able to connect with the Earth unlike any other beings."

MIKAYA and IFN1 are pumped.

IFN1 and MIKAYA: That's us!

IFN1: (*resuming her reading*) "They are Sons and Daughters of the original Mother – the Earth. The most powerful Medicine People are able to see and hear not only the sounds of the earth today but all their Ancestors that came before them."

MIKAYA: (*reading*) "Being Indigenous is about that connection, to the earth, the land."

The website's sound clip howls and the women look around.

KILAWNA: Oh Jesus Christ! Can we cut the pseudo-religious, *X-Files*-esque, magical-Indian-medium bullshit, please?

IFN1 closes the laptop, disgruntled.

IFN1: I see we have a disbeliever among us.

IFN1 and MIKAYA slowly and suspiciously look at KILAWNA.

KILAWNA: I'm not a "disbeliever." I just think there is a much wiser way to spend our time and energy than by reading websites created on Windows 98 by some honky Shaman, sitting in Wisconsin, draped in moonstones.

IFN1: But you must belieeẹevvvve in yourself, Grizzly Bear!

IFN1 reopens the laptop. A wolf's howl, a bear's growl, and extra loud flutes sound. MIKAYA barely contains her laughter.

KILAWNA: Fine. Delude yourselves into thinking that we're just a bunch of Earth whisperers.

MIKAYA: So what exactly are we then, all-knowing White Grizzly Bear?

KILAWNA: We're a race with a victim mentality, that blames the world for our problems while simultaneously asking everyone to pay for our failures.

GRIZZLY wakes.

IFN1: Woah.

KILAWNA: Yes, we got totally fucked by it all.

*KILAWNA walks over to MIKAYA and IFN1, who
are sitting on the couch, and starts throwing
the pamphlets they got at the Friendship Centre
down on them.*

KILAWNA: It's a bunch of fucking nonsense. It's a rabbit hole. It's embarrassing, it's humiliating.

KILAWNA goes back to the kitchen.

MIKAYA: You're wrong.

KILAWNA slams her dishes into the sink.

KILAWNA: Mikaya. Stop. For your own sake, please stop.

*KILAWNA goes into her bedroom and
shuts the door.*

IFN1: Must be on her moontime.

KILAWNA: I heard that!

*MIKAYA has shortness of breath. The Wind
River chills.*

ANCESTRAL VISIT

The depths. MIKAYA *has her laptop out and is streaming something. She falls in and out of consciousness.*

The Wind River gushes through the apartment and the Land Song begins.

RAVEN, SENKLIP, *and* GRIZZLY *start to shift into this world.*

MIKAYA *awakens and starts to feel her ancestral pathways. She is no longer trembling, and so she gets onto the Wind River.*

SENKLIP *enters, accompanied by the* ANCESTRAL MATRIARCHS.

ANCESTRAL MATRIARCHS: snk̓líp kʷáláʔ.

(*Mikaya, we are here.*)

Land Song.

ANCESTRAL MATRIARCHS: lút kʷtknánáks. kʷílíʔ klánʷí. k̓níáx̌.

(*You are not alone. We exist inside of you. Listen.*)

SENKLIP *howls.*

MIKAYA: Senklip.

ANCESTRAL MATRIARCHS: kʷ səcx̌stwílx̌. i tx̌tncútntət. kʷú cx̌ʷílx̌ʷált klánwí. kʷú yáʕyáʕt kʷú tkʕám.

(*You are trying to heal it. Our spirits. We, us, live in you. We are all a part of the journey.*)

SENKLIP *presences itself for* MIKAYA, *and it is the most beautiful creature she has ever seen.*

ANCESTRAL MATRIARCHS: anx̌ʷəlx̌ʷx̌ʷáltən, snk̓líp, íscx̌ʷlwístət cx̌ʷlx̌ʷált yát kákní il təmx̱ʷúláx̌tət. kʷ cx̌ʷylwís i tá təmx̌əúláx̌tət mí kʷú łcp̓lák, táłt əcmístíx̌ʷ i stłtáłtət.

(*Your existence, Mikaya, our journeys live between all worlds. You must journey through the worlds to come home, to bear witness to our truth.*)

> MIKAYA *goes to touch* SENKLIP.

MIKAYA: How...?

ANCESTRAL MATRIARCHS: i káskást łac x̌ʷílwís íl təmx̱ʷúláx̌ʷtət úł, k̓ł̓áysncútsəlx̌.

(*The Shifters travel through all worlds, connecting us, transforming us.*)

> *The drums begin to rise with the Land Song. A gust of wind blows back through the apartment.*

> *Returning from the Wind River journey,* MIKAYA *goes to sleep in her bedroom. The Land Song flows away.*

RAVEN'S LANDING

Morning in the sisters' apartment. KILAWNA
exits her room and sees that MIKAYA *is not on
the couch. She starts the coffee and heads into
the bathroom.* MIKAYA *exits her room, smells the
coffee, and starts to make breakfast for her sister.*
KILAWNA *comes out of the bathroom and gets her
coffee ready.*

MIKAYA: Morning.

KILAWNA pours a cup of coffee to go.

MIKAYA: I was going to get you...

KILAWNA: Don't have time.

KILAWNA grabs her purse and jacket.

MIKAYA: I made you breakfast.

KILAWNA: I don't have time.

KILAWNA exits out the front door and MIKAYA *is
by herself.* IFN1 *enters.*

IFN1: Breakfast!

IFN1 starts to eat. Silence.

IFN1: You got something to say?

MIKAYA, surprised, looks up at IFN1.

IFN1: Indian instinct.

*MIKAYA takes a deep breath and looks back
towards the door. A gust of the Wind River flows in.*

MIKAYA: Why is it... why do we...?

Beat.

IFN1: It hasn't always been this way, Mik.

Beat.

IFN1: Yes, we got totally fucked by it all. Colonization these past three, four hundred years has been a real punk-ass bitch. The epidemics, the genocides, the losses, it's all here.

IFN1 taps her arm, points to her head, and touches her heart.

IFN1: And it hurts. It's like these two beings pushing at one another.

Heart. Beats.

IFN1: But we gotta go deeper inside us. We can't be conditioned into just focusing on when the Settlers came and all the damage they've done. That's what they want us to be consumed by. But it's not what we need, it's not what they lived for.

Ancestral calls.

IFN1: We go back twenty thousand years and all that lives within us. They musta had some amazing victories.

War cries.

IFN1: And it's our job to remember all of it. We won some of those wars. We're still winning.

MIKAYA: We're still here.

Drums beat.

IFN1: We should go over to the Friendship Centre, it's Powwow Night, 'member?!

MIKAYA: Yeah.

Hearts.

IFN1 gets up.

IFN1: We gotta make some outfits.

MIKAYA: Outfits?

IFN1: We can't be looking like a bunch of honkies tonight.

MIKAYA makes a face.

IFN1: Reverse racism isn't a thing.

MIKAYA and IFN1 laugh.

Ancient.

Hearts.

Beating.

THE FIRE IS CALLING

KILAWNA enters the apartment, exhausted.
She plops herself down, puts on Jewel's "Foolish
Games," and relaxes on the couch.

Smoke starts to appear behind KILAWNA. It's
coming from the bathroom. It grows and plums
behind her.

KILAWNA waves her hand around her nose.

KILAWNA: What's that smell?

She starts coughing.

KILAWNA: What the hell ...

KILAWNA turns around and sees the smoke.

KILAWNA: Ohhh myyy gawwwd!

KILAWNA falls off the couch and starts crawling
towards the kitchen. She grabs the fire extinguisher
and crouch-runs to the bathroom door.

KILAWNA: It smells like a fucking Christmas craft fair in here!!!

Beat.

KILAWNA: (*going to kick the bathroom door open*) Okay:
one, two –

The moment KILAWNA's leg is in the air, IFN1 and
MIKAYA burst out of the bathroom. KILAWNA
sprays them with the fire extinguisher.

All at once, screaming:

IFN1: AHHHHHHHHHHHHH, TOOOOOOOOO
MUCCCCCCCCCH INDIAN!!!

MIKAYA: IIIIIIIIIIIII'MMMMMMMMMM
GONNNNNNNNAAAA PASSSSSSS OUT!!

KILAWNA: WHHHHHHHHHHAAAAAAT THHHHHEEEE...

> KILAWNA chases IFN1 and MIKAYA around
> the apartment, spraying them with the fire
> extinguisher. Smoke continues to pour out of
> the bathroom.
>
> All at once, screaming:

MIKAYA: PLEASE STOP!!!

IFN1: WHY???

KILAWNA: DROP AND ROLL!!!

> After one more lap around the apartment, IFN1
> opens the front door. The smoke starts to dissipate.

IFN1: Kilawna!!! Stop spraying us!

> MIKAYA is overwhelmed with the spraying and
> running, and she collapses face down on the couch.

IFN1: DON'T LET THE WHITE TAKE YOU!!!

> KILAWNA jumps over the couch and into the
> bathroom, making sure there is no fire in there. She
> emerges an instant after holding an abalone shell
> and an eagle feather.

IFN1: Woah girl! You look majestic.

KILAWNA: This looks like Wicca.

IFN1: Relax, *Charmed.*

MIKAYA: (*speaking in ṅsəlxciṅ*) xáʔx̌ʔít.

  (*Ancestors.*)

IFN1: Stigmata!

IFN1 goes to the spice rack and grabs the sage. She sprinkles it over MIKAYA.

KILAWNA: (*looking at the abalone shell and feather in her hands*) What is this?

IFN1: Smudge bowl and eagle feather.

KILAWNA: Is this what was on fire?

IFN1: Fire? There was no fire, we just got a little carried away with ceremony.

KILAWNA: Ceremony?

IFN1: Ya, we learned how to smudge tonight at the Friendship Centre, so we bought some spiritual supplies. We weren't sure how much to use so we just lit it all on fire.

KILAWNA: Jesus Christ, you two! I thought the apartment was burning.

IFN1: Nope, just two indians trying to spiritually awaken themselves.

MIKAYA comes to. She and IFN1 start miming what smudging is with the leftover spirit smoke. We see that they are both covered in white extinguisher dust, but underneath they are wearing army jackets and red bandanas around their neck.

KILAWNA: Are you okay, Mikaya?!

MIKAYA: Kilawna, we have the best news ever!

KILAWNA: Now what?

MIKAYA: We unlocked how to be real indians tonight!

KILAWNA: Real indians?

IFN1 gets right into KILAWNA's face.

IFN1: Real indians.

MIKAYA: We have to become Powwow dancers!!! We have to go dance in a Powwow!

KILAWNA: That's a really stupid fucking idea. Almost as stupid as the time you thought leaving sand in your cooch would make a pearl.

IFN1: Did it?!?

MIKAYA: Not yet.

KILAWNA: Jesus Christ.

IFN1: We were being so ridiculous with the other things.

KILAWNA: Like the fact that you two are dressed up like an homage to the Oka Crisis.

IFN1 and MIKAYA: Awesome!!!

MIKAYA: And, Kilawna, you get to be a part of the journey.

IFN1: We're road-tripping to the biggest Powwow west of the Rockies.

IFN1 and MIKAYA: KAMLOOPA!

MIKAYA: And you get to drive us there!

KILAWNA: Like hell I am.

IFN1: Oh, burn.

MIKAYA: You have to!

KILAWNA: You want me to drive you on some stupid Vision Quest to partake in some Powwow?! Mikaya, you don't even know how to freaking smudge.

IFN1: Too soon!

KILAWNA: You're just an internet indian. The both of you!

MIKAYA: I had an experience –

KILAWNA: Ya, you almost died of smoke inhalation.

IFN1: It was spirit smoke.

MIKAYA: I did not! You just –

KILAWNA: Don't try and blame this on me. If it's anyone, it's you! (*pointing to IFN1*)

IFN1: Don't you point at me, Grizzly Bear.

MIKAYA: We have to return home…

KILAWNA: Have you lost it?!

IFN1: And what if she has?

> *MIKAYA points to the direction that she thinks is home.*

MIKAYA: We need to do this. You have to believe me. We need to return home.

> *MIKAYA points her finger in the direction she thinks her Syilx Traditional Territory is.*

IFN1: You look like E.T.

MIKAYA: And this Powwow, is…, it's… (*affirmative*) it's how we become real indians. We need to go and dance.

KILAWNA: (*pointing to IFN1*) Make her drive you.

IFN1: Stop pointing at me. And, legally speaking, I am not permitted to drive in the Province of British Columbia, nor the Province of Newfoundland and Labrador.

MIKAYA: And you know I don't have an automobile permit.

IFN1: Clearly.

MIKAYA: I know this sort of thing scares you and you think you can just pretend to be white and make everything white.

KILAWNA: I don't try and make everything white.

> *IFN1 and MIKAYA smack their jackets and a plume of white fire-extinguisher dust floats off of them.*

KILAWNA: Oh, shut it.

SENKLIP starts to shift into MIKAYA. MIKAYA's heart starts to pound. She pants and yelps from the pain in SENKLIP's shoulder. RAVEN squawks. The Wind River flows.

IFN1: (*to MIKAYA*) Keep breathing.

MIKAYA nods. She breathes and exhales largely. KILAWNA looks at her sister and at IFN1.

KILAWNA: When would we leave?

IFN1: The Vision Quest starts in two moonfalls.

KILAWNA: Well, I certainly can't leave you with Number 1 over here.

IFN1: That's Indian Friend Number 1 to you, sister!

KILAWNA walks towards her bedroom hiding a smile.

KILAWNA: You've got two days to clean this place up.

MIKAYA and IFN1 look at each other and are surprised she agreed.

Just as KILAWNA is about to enter into her apartment she turns around.

KILAWNA: And another thing. HÁY ČXʷ Q̓Ə, bitches.

END OF HIBERNATION

ON THE LAND:
RETURN OF SENKLIP

Lights come up on IFN1, MIKAYA, *and* KILAWNA *in a car.* IFN1 *and* MIKAYA *are dressed like frontier colonial explorers.*

IFN1: (*finishing a joke*)... and that's why you never cook bannock topless!

> (*Note: A different line from the one above can be improvised by the actor playing* IFN1 *before each new performance and they should not tell the other performers.*)

MIKAYA: Awesome!

> KILAWNA *shakes her head.*

MIKAYA: Well, in preparation for the journey, we learned some road-trip songs.

> IFN1 *passes* MIKAYA *her ukulele.*

KILAWNA: I guess those lessons we took as kids will be put to some use.

> MIKAYA *plays the first verse of Stan Rogers's 1981 song "Northwest Passage," with* IFN1 *attempting harmony.*

KILAWNA: (*when the word "savage" in the line "A land so wild and savage" comes in*) What the fuck is that?

> MIKAYA *big-teeth grins and stares directly at* KILAWNA.

IFN1: Wasn't Stan Rogers Native... Blackfoot or something? No? Well no need to sploosh. We've got more.

MIKAYA *starts playing the next song and* IFN1 *accompanies her on the harmonica. It's the folk song "The Log Driver's Waltz," written by Wade Hemsworth. While playing,* MIKAYA *and* IFN1 *start waltzing in their seats and singing like what they think old British women would sound like. They get through the first verse and chorus, ending on "The log driver's waltz pleases girls completely" before* KILAWNA *interrupts them.*

KILAWNA: No.

MIKAYA *and* IFN1 *sing the first verse from The Travellers' 1955 "Canadianized" version of the 1940 U.S. folk song "This Land Is Your Land" by Woody Guthrie.*

MIKAYA: Take it away, Shakira!

IFN1 *sings the song's second verse, imitating the vocal and dance style of pop star Shakira.*

KILAWNA: Are you serious?

MIKAYA: Tough crowd.

IFN1: Well what did you come to the party with? Nish teaching says you never show up empty-handed.

MIKAYA: Yeeeeaaaah, whatchu got, sis?

KILAWNA: Absolutely nothing.

MIKAYA: C'mon, we didn't take those uke lessons for years for nothing.

KILAWNA: Remember our teacher who was super obsessed with Tom Petty?

MIKAYA: Oh my god, yes. Whenever we were late, he would start singing "The waiiiiiiting is the hardest part."

MIKAYA *starts playing on the ukulele an acoustic version of Tom Petty and the Heartbreakers' 1989 hit "I Won't Back Down."*

KILAWNA *smiles and remembers, then hesitantly joins in on the second verse, starting with "Well I won't back down ...," singing under her breath.*

IFN1 *joins in and the three women sing the chorus together. The Ancestral sounds accompany them.* MIKAYA *strums us out.*

KILAWNA: I wish we could've left earlier. I don't like driving at night.

MIKAYA: We tried, but we had stuff to do.

KILAWNA: You could've packed the night before.

MIKAYA: We did.

KILAWNA: What were you doing then?

IFN1: Cultural stuff.

KILAWNA *makes a discerning face.*

MIKAYA: Yeahhhhh, cultural stuff.

KILAWNA: Does "cultural stuff" include putting together your colonial frontier outfits?

IFN1: Hey! I'm Simon Fraser.

MIKAYA: Ya, and I'm... his settler friend.

KILAWNA: You don't always have to always wear ridiculous outfits to experience something, you morons.

IFN1: We weren't working on these outfits last night. We were working on –

MIKAYA *quickly shushes* IFN1 *and shakes her head.*

MIKAYA: Anyways, you're one to talk about ridiculous outfits. You were the one obsessed with Laura Ingalls and dressing like a colonial woman when we were younger.

KILAWNA: I was not.

MIKAYA: Yes you were! Remember that time we went to Pennsylvania as a family and we were in Amish country and you begged Mom and Dad to buy you an apron and a bonnet?

KILAWNA: That did not happen!

MIKAYA: Maybe you Pandora's boxed that shit but you did. Mom got you a white bonnet and an apron from the Amish women and you wore it everywhere for the rest of the trip. Out to dinner, to the amusement park… you even slept in it!

KILAWNA remembers.

KILAWNA: Oh my god.

IFN1: Your parents sound like legends.

MIKAYA: They are.

KILAWNA: I did, I wore it everywhere.

MIKAYA starts rummaging around in her bag.

IFN1: Okay, okay, okay, okay. Now, I don't think we need to explicitly say it, but I don't want to rob us of this moment. You're telling me that Kilawna spent a significant portion of her childhood dressing up and fantasizing about becoming a ˉHwiiiiiiite woman?

KILAWNA is so embarrassed.

KILAWNA: Yes! I dreamed of being a Hwiiiiiiite woman.

MIKAYA: And now we can all relive the GLORY!

MIKAYA reveals a white bonnet. IFN1 sticks her head out the window.

IFN1: THANK YOU, ANCESTORS, I LOVE YOU!

KILAWNA: (*to* MIKAYA) Where did you find that?

MIKAYA: I couldn't find the original so I got you a new one.

KILAWNA: I am not putting that thing on.

IFN1: Oh c'mon. All in all, when you look at it, maybe you were just into Laura Ingalls. She was a badass boss bitch.

MIKAYA and KILAWNA: (*in unison*) TRUTH!

IFN1: It could be like an act of reclamation.

KILAWNA: I don't think that's how that works.

MIKAYA: Sure it can.

IFN1: Ya, it's like you're wearing it as an indian now, not dreaming of being some half-pint.

KILAWNA: That's such a terrible idea it might be true.

IFN1: (*encouraging* KILAWNA) Let's just plop it on and see what happens.

> *On her ukulele,* MIKAYA *starts playing the opening tune to the* TV *show* Little House on the Prairie *("The Little House," written by David Rose).* IFN1 *dramatically soars the bonnet over and onto* KILAWNA's *head; it's giant.*

MIKAYA: How's it feel?

IFN1: Ya! What's happening in there?!

KILAWNA: Well it's sort of a mix of things: humiliation, depression, and childhood nostalgia.

IFN1: So like a regular day, I guess. Awesome.

> *The Wind River forks.*

KILAWNA: Can someone check their phone to make sure that we're on the right road?

IFN1: I can feel we're going in the right direction, Laura.

MIKAYA: Ya, me too. We don't need no map.

IFN1 leans over MIKAYA and screams out the window.

IFN1: TO THE MOTHERLAAAAAANDS!!!

MIKAYA laughs and also sticks her head out the window.

MIKAYA: The Motherlaaaaands!!!

MIKAYA grabs her phone.

MIKAYA: (*screaming*) I'm an indian!!!

Caught up in the moment, MIKAYA throws her phone out the window and we hear it smash. IFN1 and KILAWNA are shocked.

IFN1: YOOOOO. Too faaaaar.

KILAWNA: What the shit, Mikaya?!

MIKAYA: (*snapping out of it*) Oh my gawd.

MIKAYA pops her head out the window and looks back at her phone. She sits back down and stares out front.

IFN1: Gone.

KILAWNA: Gone.

MIKAYA: I don't know what just happened there.

MIKAYA starts to breathe heavy and fast.

KILAWNA: That was dumb.

IFN1: Cool it, Nellie. You okay, Mikaya?

MIKAYA closes her eyes.

MIKAYA: (*in n̓səl̓xcin̓, without any accent*) əɬcxʷuy ki̲_citxʷ. Return home.

KILAWNA: What was that?

> *MIKAYA's breathing starts to return to normal and she opens her eyes. Ancestral echoes. MIKAYA looks at the Wind Rivers channelling towards her.*

MIKAYA: It's beautiful out here.

IFNI: Holeh, is it ever gooder out here.

> *IFNI pulls out a bag of Hawkins Cheezies. Her fingers and face begin to turn toxic orange, covered in cheesy dust. IFNI offers some to KILAWNA.*

KILAWNA: Ya, right.

IFNI: C'mon, Grizzly Bear, this is a part of the journey of becoming a real indian.

KILAWNA: (*taking one Cheezie*) Fine.

> *SENKLIP is running on the river towards MIKAYA.*

MIKAYA: What... what is that?

KILAWNA: Hot dang, this shit is good.

IFNI: Right?!

> *KILAWNA and IFNI stuff a bunch of Cheezies into their mouths. MIKAYA sees something; she sits to attention, rolls down her window, and sees SENKLIP. We hear the faint sound of the ANCESTRAL MATRIARCHS. MIKAYA points at SENKLIP; she tries to speak but can only yelp.*

MIKAYA: (*attempting to utter "Kilawna"*) Kil-pfffffffft-ki...

> *SENKLIP rushes to MIKAYA. IFNI sees something and attempts to scream but is choking on the Cheezies.*

KILAWNA: Stop fucking around, you tw–

SENKLIP *leaps into this world.*

The three in unison:

KILAWNA: AHHHHHHHHHHHHHHHHHHH!!!

MIKAYA: Seeeeeeeennnnnnnnnkliiiiipppp!!!

IFN1: Koooooocccooooooouuuuuuummmmmmm!!!

On the Wind River, SENKLIP *crashes and channels into* MIKAYA. *In the car,* KILAWNA *attempts to grab the wheel, but her hands are too covered in Cheezie dust to get a firm grip. She hits* SENKLIP, *making impact with its shoulder, and it goes flying up into the darkness. The car starts swerving at high speed.*

KILAWNA *and* IFN1: Shiiiiiitttttttt!

KILAWNA *slams on the breaks and the woman all heave forward until the seatbelts stop them.*

The Wind River forks back into one.

MIKAYA *doesn't make a sound until the car stops; she then screams and grabs for her shoulder.*

MIKAYA: Ahhhhhhhhhhhhhhhhhhhrrrrghhhhhhhh.

KILAWNA: Is everyone okay?!

IFN1 *nods.* MIKAYA *stares ahead, alive.*

KILAWNA: Mikaya, are you okay?!?!

MIKAYA *slowly nods.* KILAWNA *gets out of the car.* IFN1 *also gets out, taking the Cheezies with her.* MIKAYA *remains.* KILAWNA *squats down and has a look at the front end of the car.*

Growls.

KILAWNA: We lost the light.

RAVEN squawks.

IFN1: Weird.

IFN1 is loudly munching on the Cheezies and offers them to KILAWNA. KILAWNA knocks the bag out of IFN1's hands and the Cheezies all spill out onto the ground.

IFN1: Why'd you do that?!

KILAWNA: We got into an accident because of those fucking Cheezies.

IFN1: Hawkins. Never. Hurt us!!!

MIKAYA exits the car and looks up the Wind River.

IFN1: Mikaya! Your sister has gone batshit fucking ridiculous.

MIKAYA doesn't hear them.

IFN1: Mikaya! Your sister is blaming the Cheezies, when it was her white-woman bonnet that made us hit that –

KILAWNA: YOU said this was an act of reclamation!

MIKAYA comes back to the road.

MIKAYA: It was a Coyote.

KILAWNA: What?

MIKAYA: And it didn't die.

IFN1: Pardon you?

MIKAYA: Something died out there but it wasn't the coyote.

IFN1 walks into MIKAYA's face.

IFN1: She's obviously concussed.

KILAWNA: Mikaya, I think you should sit down.

MIKAYA immediately sits where she is standing.

KILAWNA: I meant, like, in the car or something.

The Land speaks and the Wind River forks again.

IFN1: Where are we?

KILAWNA: Outside.

MIKAYA: (*uttering the n̓səlx̌cin̓ word meaning "the greatest and oldest members of the family"*) K̓awiwelx.

> *KILAWNA goes into the car and grabs her phone. She tries to make a call.*

KILAWNA: Of course there is no service.

> *KILAWNA shakes her head.*

MIKAYA: We should camp the night here.

> *Howls.*

KILAWNA: Excuse me?

> *RAVEN flies into SENKLIP's river.*

IFN1: Yes!!!

MIKAYA: Kilawna, we are here.

KILAWNA: Where? I thought Powwows had people.

MIKAYA: Home, our Territory, Syilx, the Motherland.

> *KILAWNA stops and takes that in. IFN1 breathes it in, and wipes some Cheezie dust from her face.*

IFN1: Who votes that we set up camp here?!

> *MIKAYA and IFN1 raise their hands immediately.*

IFN1: Motion passes: Camp Coyote Killers commence!

MIKAYA *howls like* SENKLIP *and* IFNI *honks like* RAVEN. *They are incredibly enthusiastic as they set up camp, dancing and howling and wildly jumping around.*

EMBODIED LAND

*Camp Coyote Killers is magnificent. The three
women are sitting on stumps around their fire
with a pop-up tent behind them.* KILAWNA *is still
wearing the bonnet.*

IFN1: Well that went surprisingly smooth.

MIKAYA: Ya! Who says we're terrible indians?

KILAWNA: I do.

MIKAYA: Not anymore!

> KILAWNA *walks around camp searching
> for service.*

KILAWNA: Is anyone getting any service here?

IFN1: You mean twenty feet from where we left the car and had
no service, has it changed since then?

Beat.

IFN1: No, it hasn't changed. Mikaya has no phone, I have no
service, and the light is still out. I've got the longest legs of us
all so I will go on a Vision Quest at daybreak to get us service.

MIKAYA: Vision Quest?

IFN1: When in Rome...

Beat.

KILAWNA: What time is the Powwow tomorrow?

MIKAYA: Grand Entry is at 11 a.m.

KILAWNA: Heh? Grand Entry?

MIKAYA: From what I gathered, "Grand Entry" is when everyone
enters the park... um... dance... uh... place like a parade.

MIKAYA's breath starts to go.

IFN1: Oh my gaaaaawwd, a parade?! "Grand Entry" is when the dancers are called into the grounds in a good way. The dancers follow the Head Dancers, respected leaders. The drumming is central to the entire event. It is the heartbeat of the people, the Land, us.

> *MIKAYA and KILAWNA are surprised at IFN1's knowledge. IFN1 grabs a single sheet of paper out of her pocket.*

IFN1: Or at least that's what it says on my "Powwow 101" printout.

KILAWNA: Gimmie that.

> *KILAWNA starts to read it.*

KILAWNA: So you two are going to "dance" behind these respected people?

IFN1: Sure.

KILAWNA: It doesn't say anything about...

MIKAYA: About what?

KILAWNA: ... how you do it?

IFN1: Enter?

KILAWNA: Any of it. What are you wearing? Do you even know how to dance?

IFN1: It's just in us. I think when we hit the floor it's just going to come to us.

> *IFN1 shimmies her chest.*

MIKAYA: Yeah, and I think what she also means is that we've done the research.

KILAWNA: Really?

MIKAYA: We saw those dancers at the Friendship Centre.

KILAWNA: And that has made you expert Powwowers?

MIKAYA: For sure. We have some killer outfits.

IFN1: We were working on them this morning.

MIKAYA: That's what was taking us so long.

KILAWNA: What does yours look like, Mikaya?

IFN1: Awesome! It's impressive, feastly. Mikaya, go put yours on! This is your super-indian moment, on the Motherlands, outside, right after we just…

> *IFN1 gestures and makes the North American Indian Sign Language sign for "river." RAVEN honks. IFN1 gets in the Wind River.*

KILAWNA: Ya, Mikaya, let's see it.

MIKAYA: Okay.

> *MIKAYA gets off her stump and enters the tent. The ANCESTOR presences herself through RAVEN, THEN IFN1, and sits at the fire with KILAWNA.*

KILAWNA: What was that?

IFN1 (*shifting into*) ANCESTOR: (*teasingly*) Secret.

KILAWNA: C'mon, tell me.

> *The ANCESTOR gestures and takes out her medicine pouch. She lays some tobacco on the ground.*

KILAWNA: And what was that?

IFN1 | ANCESTOR: Slow down, Grizzly Bear.

> *She makes the sign for "Slow down."*

KILAWNA: You look like an indian from one of those old movies.

IFN1 | ANCESTOR: It's Indian Sign Language.

KILAWNA: Is that even a thing?

IFN1 | ANCESTOR: When the Settlers first came, they couldn't speak our languages. They didn't understand us. How could they? They thought we were just making these gestures that didn't have any meaning. (*breath*) We knew what we were doing. We have complex and sophisticated ways of communicating, physically. We have hundreds of languages to navigate, trade, and live with, so we created a language to be with each other.

> *The Wind River makes the fire and bushes dance. The silence of thought. We hear a faint drumming and the wind carries the gentle hum of the Land Song.*

> *A grizzly* CUB *presences itself in* KILAWNA.

KILAWNA | CUB: Can you teach me some?

IFN1 | ANCESTOR: Here are some things we use every day.

> IFN1 | ANCESTOR *raises her right hand below her shoulder, palm facing down; she flips it and moves it to her right. This means "No."* KILAWNA | CUB *mimics her.*

KILAWNA | CUB: "No."

> IFN1 | ANCESTOR *moves her right hand, index finger out, in a downward motion.*

IFN1 | ANCESTOR: "Yes."

KILAWNA | CUB: (*mimicking her*) "Yes."

> *The* CUB *giggles.*

> IFN1 | ANCESTOR *moves her right hand down her left arm in a tapping motion.*

IFN1 | ANCESTOR: "Indian."

Beat. The CUB *takes her time and puts her paw on her own arm.*

KILAWNA | CUB: "Indian."

IFN1 | ANCESTOR places her left hand, palm down, at her heart and moves her left arm out until it is almost completely extended.

IFN1 | ANCESTOR: "Good."

IFN1 | ANCESTOR makes a fist over her heart with her left hand and makes a downward motion, releasing the fist.

IFN1 | ANCESTOR: "Bad."

KILAWNA | CUB goes through the two last movements.

KILAWNA | CUB: "Good... Bad."

IFN1 | ANCESTOR motions a sequence.

KILAWNA | CUB: What was that?

IFN1 | ANCESTOR: "Crazy white people."

IFN1 | ANCESTOR laughs and the CUB runs into the woods. The ANCESTRAL MATRIARCH looks at KILAWNA.

KILAWNA: What?

IFN1 | ANCESTOR: You look like an indian.

As she speaks, IFN1 | ANCESTOR makes the Native American Indian Sign Language gesture for "Indian": she taps her left arm with her right hand three times, starting at her elbow, moving down her arm.

KILAWNA: You're being dumb.

IFN1 | ANCESTOR: Kilawna, you are Grizzly Bear.

*GRIZZLY is seen for the first time. We hear
the faint, comforting songs of the ANCESTRAL
MATRIARCHS. Branches break like someone
is walking into the woods. For the first time,
KILAWNA thinks she hears something.*

IFN1 | ANCESTOR: Sometimes we feel alone. I have felt very
alone. But try to remember we are always with you,
Grizzly Bear.

KILAWNA: When were you alone?

*The Wind River forks and the ANCESTOR floats
on, the question is answered downriver. We hear
a loud crash coming from the tent. IFN1 makes a
Ravenesque audible cry.*

KILAWNA: Are you okay in there?

MIKAYA: (*from the tent*) Yep, just struggling with putting on my
Powwow clothes.

IFN1: Metaphor.

KILAWNA: Well do you want any help?

IFN1: You?! Help her?! With being an indian?

KILAWNA: You're not wrong.

IFN1: Just come out, it'll be great!

MIKAYA: (*stepping out*) Please remember that it's not entirely
done, so…

*MIKAYA is wearing a long skirt with a hundred
curled tuna-can lids, bright dollar-store feathers,
and curly ribbons. Her top is a fleece blanket
bearing the image of a wolf and a sexualized
Indigenous woman; attached are what look like
party streamers. She's wearing a beanie hat where,
instead of a propeller, there are a feather and a
plush doll of a miniature Indigenous woman.*

She is holding a snare drum, with drum sticks
inserted in her gun-holster belt.

IFN1: Decisions have been made.

MIKAYA: What?

KILAWNA is in shock.

IFN1: Do a little twirl.

MIKAYA does.

KILAWNA: Is that a white woman, dressed as a Native woman, heavy-panting over a bunch of wolves?

MIKAYA: ... Yes ...

KILAWNA: Do you have an indian doll hanging off your head?

MIKAYA: ... Yes ...

KILAWNA: Mikaya, she looks like she's being hanged.

MIKAYA: Right, okay, I can take that one off.

IFN1: Let's not start editing just yet.

MIKAYA: Okay.

GRIZZLY starts sniffing the air.

KILAWNA: What's that smell?

IFN1: Outside stuff?

KILAWNA: Smells like... fish...

IFN1: (*spreading her legs and wafting the air upwards*) I'm not on my moontime.

MIKAYA: Is it the tuna cans on my skirt?

KILAWNA: Yes, it is. It is the tuna cans on your skirt, Mikaya.

MIKAYA: I really thought I cleaned them enough. Jingle dresses are made from tobacco-can lids, but I didn't have any.

IFN1: This thing just keeps on giving.

MIKAYA: Too much?

Beat.

MIKAYA: Ohhhh, not enough.

KILAWNA: Somehow both, I think.

MIKAYA starts to pant.

IFN1: What's with the snare drum?

MIKAYA grabs a stick and bangs on the drum.

MIKAYA: Killing it with my beats?

IFN1: Proud of you.

GRIZZLY starts to growl.

IFN1: Can I put mine on now?

MIKAYA: Please!

IFN1 enters the tent. KILAWNA gets up and reaches into her purse, grabs a cigarette, and goes to light it.

MIKAYA: What are you doing?

KILAWNA: What does it look like?

MIKAYA: You smoke?!

KILAWNA: It's traditional.

MIKAYA: You're a piece of work.

KILAWNA looks at MIKAYA and what she is wearing.

MIKAYA: I acknowledge that at this particular moment, it's a bit rich coming from me, but *smoking*? Have you lost it?

KILAWNA: I have a cigarette once in a while, kill me.

KILAWNA's *lighter won't work and she throws the cigarette.*

KILAWNA: I hate this place.

The Wind River carries in SENKLIP *and* GRIZZLY.

KILAWNA: (*looking at* MIKAYA) You look like a fool.

GRIZZLY *grounds itself.*

KILAWNA: I thought that I could do this little cultural charade with you, but I didn't think it would be so idiotic. I can't even look at you.

MIKAYA: What? What can't you look at?!

KILAWNA: Your pseudo-indian, Ancestral, Mother-Earth connection wannabe bullshit.

SENKLIP *comes to the fire beside* MIKAYA.
GRIZZLY *gets up in agitation.*

MIKAYA: You're just jealous that I'm a better indian than you!

SENKLIP *howls.*

KILAWNA: You're an embarrassment, Mikaya.

MIKAYA: Why, because I actually give a shit?

KILAWNA: Don't delude yourself into thinking that you are somehow better than me. You're the worst fucking indian in the entire world. Or maybe you are the best because you think playing bingo is being an indian.

MIKAYA: If you hate being an indian so much why did you even come?!

KILAWNA: Your desperation is palpable, Mikaya.

GRIZZLY *bluff charges at* SENKLIP.

MIKAYA: You fucking hate yourself, Kilawna!!!

KILAWNA gets up in MIKAYA's face, grabs her hat,
and throws it into the fire.

GRIZZLY stands fully upright, swipes and
hits SENKLIP.

KILAWNA: GROOOOOOWLLLLLL!!!

MIKAYA: AHHHHHHHRGGGGHHHHHOOOOO-
WWWLLLLL!!!

SENKLIP falls to the ground. GRIZZLY gives one
last growl at the downed SENKLIP.

KILAWNA: RAAAAAAAAAAAAOOOOORRRHHHHR!!!

MIKAYA is enraged. Everything is coming out of
her: she gnarls and collapses to her hands and
knees. SENKLIP barks and bitches. GRIZZLY slightly
retreats back. RAVEN squawks.

IFN1 sticks her head out of the tent. KILAWNA
moves towards her.

MIKAYA: Don't touch me!!!

SENKLIP howls.

MIKAYA: I can't sleep and when I do I see things. (*screaming the*
ṅsəlxciṅ word for "older sister") łkíkxaʔ!

IFN1: Woah.

MIKAYA slowly starts to get up from her hands
and knees.

MIKAYA: I can't breathe a lot of the time. I'm scared of being...
I'm scared of being. My body feels like it's being ripped apart
and you keep asking me to ignore it. I close my eyes and I'm
awake, so I don't want to shut my eyes because I'm terrified
of what's inside me. My own body is trying to eradicate me.
In a world that already doesn't want me, my own body is
killing me! And you can make fun of me, and you can scoff

at everything I'm trying to do, but at least I'm facing it. I am trying to face our truth, Kilawna!

GRIZZLY *sits back.*

MIKAYA: Something is happening. I'm not sad anymore, if anything I'm angry... I am angry... I'M SO ANGRY!!!

SENKLIP *howls.*

MIKAYA: I'm trying to bear witness to myself, it's something I've neglected to do my entire life. Was it that dream or vision... I don't know! It's hard for me to believe what's happening, but denying it is going to kill me, it's going to kill us all.

Ancestral cries.

MIKAYA: Something did die out on that road, but it wasn't the Coyote...

GRIZZLY *huffs.* RAVEN *swoops.*

IFN1: I've felt that loneliness, that broken feeling on the inside. That space where we know something should be. That intangible river that used to connect us to something more... to everything. I understand, Mikaya. I'm not sure how, but I see you. I see what's happening. I want my Mothers, my Sisters, my People to...

IFN1 makes the gesture for "to connect": with both hands at waist level, index fingers pointing forwards and remaining fingers bent, she brings her hands together until the index fingers touch.

KILAWNA: We are all alone.

IFN1: We are not alone! Look around, Kilawna. Your Ancestors are here, on your Land, with you.

GRIZZLY *and* SENKLIP *retreat.*

IFN1: Now, can I get a drum roll, please?

MIKAYA reluctantly beats her snare.

IFN1: Now, I went much more traditional than Mikaya's more contemporary ensemble.

RAVEN jumps.

RAVEN | IFN1 jumps up on a stump and starts voguing. Her outfit is simple: just three tiny pieces of buckskin (one displaying hand-painted images and barely covering her lower half), a chest plate top made out of sticks. In some terrifying way, it's pretty spectacular. But KILAWNA is making the gesture for "bad" repeatedly.

KILAWNA: What is going on with your bottom thing?

IFN1: Oh. I drew the story of "Two Suns Rising," kind of an homage to you and Mikaya.

KILAWNA: It looks like an angry vagina.

IFN1: Accurate, then.

KILAWNA: You can't wear that to the Powwow. It's offensive.

MIKAYA: Yes she can! She's Indigenous. WE are Indigenous.

Growls.

KILAWNA: We are not well. I think we should go home.

IFN1: Whaaaat?!

Barks.

MIKAYA: We are not going home!!!

KILAWNA: Look how messed up we are. What do you think is going to happen when we get to the fucking Powwow and nobody knows what to do?

IFN1: I have the handout!

MIKAYA: I need you to listen!!!

The Wind River rushes in and we hear SENKLIP
howl from the forest. It rattles all their bones. The
Worlds are starting to collide.

MIKAYA: Can we please just go to sleep so we can go to this
fucking Powwow in the morning!!!

IFN1: You got it, Chief. (*gesturing for* KILAWNA *to enter the tent*)
Kilawna.

> GRIZZLY *follows, then* MIKAYA, *then* SENKLIP.
> IFN1 *turns around and we see that she is wearing*
> *a beaded G-string. Just before she enters the tent,*
> IFN1 *smacks her own ass and raises her fist to the*
> *air;* RAVEN *lands on the tent.*

IFN1: Fuck, I love this place.

The Wind River puts the fire out.

Beating.

Drums.

Call.

LANDING TOGETHER

Morning light has found KILAWNA, MIKAYA, *and*
IFN1. *A warm wind smelling of sage and sweetgrass
grabs us. They clean up the campsite and climb
back into the car.*

Drums.

Drums...

Drumming...

*They arrive at the Powwow grounds and it's a
spiritual and cultural battlefield. The sound is
blinding. The drum groups' vocables shake the
women. They are overwhelmed.*

*They look up and out at the Sun through the
opening of the Arbour, the portal and mouth of the
Wind River. The currents are strong.* KILAWNA,
MIKAYA, *and* IFN1 *bear witness to the power of
their people, dancing, laughing, and living.*

MIKAYA: It's really loud.

IFN1: I still think we should've stopped at that restaurant Señor
Frog's.

KILAWNA: Jesus Christ.

IFN1: This town has not one but two of them!

MIKAYA: *¡Ay, caramba!*

IFN1: Two!!!

*MIKAYA and IFN1 nod in unison. The drum group
finishes their song, but we still feel the drum.*

IFN1: Where's the men's traditional at?

MIKAYA: Huh, why?

IFN1: Sometimes you can catch a little peekaboo butt action.

KILAWNA and MIKAYA make eye contact for the first time in a while.

IFN1: (*her breath beginning to leave her*) I... uhh... I don't think I...

MIKAYA: You okay?

KILAWNA: I gotta... I gotta...

KILAWNA leaves MIKAYA and IFN1 in this world.

IFN1 Where is she going?!

KILAWNA travels through time and space on the Wind River. The River has forked and KILAWNA is sitting at the Arbour, in front of the fire from last night.

IFN1: Lotta indians here...

MIKAYA: I feel you.

IFN1: I haven't seen so many since...

MIKAYA: The Friendship Centre?

IFN1: Since being in foster care.

Children.

Cries.

The Wind River flows back and pulls IFN1 with it.

MIKAYA and KILAWNA: What?

IFN1: Don't look at me like that!

Heartbeat.

KILAWNA and MIKAYA: I'm... I'm sorry...?

IFN1: Jesus Christ, for what? What are you sorry for?

MIKAYA: That you had to be –

IFN1: – in foster care? People don't get it. They are either scared of me or they pity me.

A cry from RAVEN.

IFN1: Foster care sucked. Fuck, it sucked. But you know what else sucks? You and your sister shitting all over each other. You tear each other apart.

MIKAYA watches as the biggest RAVEN she's ever seen soars around the portal, the opening of the Arbour.

KILAWNA and **MIKAYA:** I don't want it to be like this…

RAVEN | IFN1: (*soaring*) I've flown alone most of my life and I've met a lot of birds, but you two have the power to heal things. Your connection is where your powers live. Believe in it.

RAVEN lands.

RAVEN | IFN1: Don't let that world take anything more from us. You two are one; heal it.

RAVEN | IFN1 flies off.

KILAWNA and MIKAYA, in unison:

KILAWNA: Whaa…?

MIKAYA: Where are you going?!?

The Wind River flows forward and brings KILAWNA back to the Arbour. MIKAYA holds her wounds; they hurt. She realizes that people have little areas where they sit and tries to find her space. Among the thousands of people, KILAWNA spots her sister from across the Arbour.

KILAWNA: You can do this.

*MIKAYA starts to pull her Powwow clothes from
her backpack. They look nothing like what the
other women are wearing; hers are covered in
dust, mud, and shame. Her breath starts to go and
she rubs her hands. She starts to fumble and drops
her clothes.*

KILAWNA: C'mon, Mikaya, c'mon, believe. You can do this.

*MIKAYA's bones are rattling. The heartbeat of the
Land is slamming against her. The Wind River
engulfs her, and she collapses under the current.*

MIKAYA: I... I can't...

*GRIZZLY shifts towards KILAWNA. SENKLIP shifts
towards MIKAYA. MIKAYA gasps for breath.*

MIKAYA: KILAWNA!!!

KILAWNA stands.

KILAWNA: MIKAYA!!!

*KILAWNA joins GRIZZLY on the Wind River and
transforms.*

MIKAYA: I can do this, I can do this. I am a strong and powerful
Indigenous woman... I am a strong and powerful Indigenous
woman...

*SENKLIP enters MIKAYA, transforming her.
GRIZZLY | KILAWNA rushes to her sister.*

*MIKAYA is overwhelmed with the transformation
and starts to collapse. GRIZZLY | KILAWNA and
SENKLIP MIKAYA see one another.*

MIKAYA: GRIZZLY KILAWNA!!!

GRIZZLY | KILAWNA catches SENKLIP | MIKAYA.

GRIZZLY | KILAWNA: SENKLIP!!!

Bang.

Dimensions shift, time suspends, and everything exists in this moment.

GRIZZLY *catches* SENKLIP *before it hits the ground and they experience their full selves for the very first time.*

The ANCESTRAL MATRIARCHS *speak through the* SHIFTERS.

GRIZZLY | KILAWNA: I'm here. I see you. Finally.

SENKLIP | MIKAYA *bears a smile and looks into* GRIZZLY | KILAWNA*'s eyes.*

SENKLIP | MIKAYA: I see them, us. The women. All of us. It's extraordinary.

GRIZZLY | KILAWNA *and the* ANCESTRAL MATRIARCHS *are speaking blood to blood.*

ANCESTRAL MATRIARCHS: (*in ṅsəɬxciṅ*) kʷú áláʔ. kʷúmənímɬtət klánwí, sənk̓lp, kʷú mənímɬtət klánwí, kíláwnáʔ.

(*We are here. We are you, Senklip Mikaya. We are you, Grizzly Kilawna.*)

All of our ANCESTORS *have arrived.*

GRIZZLY | KILAWNA: It's our time, sisters. We are so much, Senklip. We always have been, there is so much love. It is time to rise and be seen for everything we are. This is who we're meant to be.

GRIZZLY | KILAWNA *embraces* SENKLIP | MIKAYA.

GRIZZLY | KILAWNA: Somewhere between this world and the last...

SENKLIP | MIKAYA: (*in ṅsəɬxciṅ*) lút nyáʕíp kʷú tə knánáqs. kúcʔúllús nyáʕíp i kl̓xáʔx̌ítət.

(*We are never alone. Together forever with the Ancestors.*)

The sounds of the Ancestral Land Song and of the Powwow collide.

Bang.

The dimensions shift and Wind River delivers the women fully at the grounds. GRIZZLY | KILAWNA *and* SENKLIP | MIKAYA *hear a loud* RAVEN *honking as* IFNI *flies towards them. She signs "It's our time": rotating her right hand counterclockwise with the palm down, then raising two fists with index fingers pointed out up into the air, alternating between one and the other.*

GRIZZLY | KILAWNA: I got something for the both of you.

GRIZZLY | KILAWNA *gifts the most beautiful yolks from her regalia to* MIKAYA *and* IFNI *and hands one to each of them.* IFNI *is bursting with joy.*

SENKLIP | MIKAYA: Don't you get one?

GRIZZLY | KILAWNA: I am here to bear witness to you…

She makes the North American Indian Sign Language gesture for "to bear witness": she points to her eyes with her right hand and then moves her hand outwards. She then touches her heart.

GRIZZLY | KILAWNA: … something I am learning to do.

A RAVEN's *cry.*

GRIZZLY | KILAWNA: What is your name, friend?

RAVEN SQUAWKS.

EDITH: My name is Edith.

MIKAYA *makes the sign for "thank you": with both hands palm down, she makes a wavelike motion downwards and to the right.*

SENKLIP | MIKAYA: Thank you, sister.

EDITH *is filled with love and returns the gesture*
for "thank you." The beings embrace.

SENKLIP | MIKAYA: (*to* GRIZZLY | KILAWNA) Are you coming?

GRIZZLY | KILAWNA: Grizzly Bears can't dance.

SENKLIP | MIKAYA *and* RAVEN *enter the*
grounds onto the Land with the dancers and our
ANCESTORS.

GRIZZLY | KILAWNA : Go, my cubs.

The Wind River flows.

GRIZZLY | KILAWNA: (*in n̓səlxcin̓*) lút nyáʕíp kʷú ɫə knánáqs.
kúcʔúllús nyáʕíp i kl̓x̌áʔx̌ítət.

(*We are never alone. Together forever with the Ancestors.*)

The Land gives KILAWNA *breath and peace as she*
experiences a happiness she's never felt before.

Our ANCESTORS *sing for us.*

NO END

FIRE ZINE!
A KAMLOOPA STUDY BUDDY

A Resource for *Kamloopa:*
An Indigenous Matriarch Story
by Kim Senklip Harvey
with the Fire Company

by Miki Wolf

Protocols for the Indigenous Artistic Ceremony *Kamloopa*

First, Indigenous Protocol. Period. End of story.

Ha ha ha, but seriously, like, we're stating it's Indigenous artistic ceremony
Protocol – that should be enough and that alone should be respected. I've
had the fortune and privilege of participating in ceremony and in the
Indigenous paradigm, and questioning that would be extremely
disrespectful. It makes me cringe thinking about questioning a Knowledge
Holder of a Longhouse or Sweat Lodge or any ceremony. #Shudder #Barf

For Indigenous Sovereignty to occur I understand that Settlers need to
understand Indigeneity, but I will say this: I have a Ph.D. in Whiteness. I've
been studying Settler Eurocentricity my entire life, I live under Settler
oppression all of the time, so I've put my time in doing the work, research,
lived experiences, and detailed studies of why I'm positioned in society
where I am.

So, I offer everyone to do an inventory of where their level of understanding
is with regards to Indigenous world views, ceremony, historical and
precolonial paradigms of thoughts, and everything beyond. Then, I offer you
consider how you make your requests from Indigenous peoples or make
potentially oppressive comments towards Indigenous Peoples who continue
to live under siege of Settler and white supremacy.

After that inventory, I would make another offer, that as a Settler, you take
time, significant time, to listen and listen and listen and experience and
experience and experience before you speak, and that maybe you use your
Settler power that currently is wielded against us to actually hold space for
Indigenous Peoples to engage and be given voice, instead of you taking
more space.

If you feel the need to speak or be given voice before, above, or louder than
Indigenous people about the ceremony, then you are actively continuing to
use your Settler power to silence, take space, and harm Indigenous Peoples,
and I think you've missed the invitation, the offer, the opportunity here.

Settlers have oppressively positioned themselves in this theatrical context to have some presumed kind of academic and or artistic "authority" over Indigenous Peoples. Historically and contemporarily that might be permissible protocol in Canadian theatre – but this is not that. This is Indigenous artistic ceremony, so I suggest that you take an inventory again of why you think you have been given authority, permission, or entitlement to speak, critique, or position yourselves over Indigenous Matriarchs creating Indigenous artistic ceremony.

We're not looking for comparative analysis with Canadian Theatre and we're not seeking comparative experiential analysis with Canadian Theatre that has told Indigenous stories. We are inviting you to come and bear witness and participate in Indigenous artistic ceremony, to learn what that means, and not aggressively assert Settler power over us. At the top of the *Kamloopa* ceremony, we will share with you how to bear witness, and we hope you can embody the values of respect, humility, courage, wisdom, trust, love, and honesty as we journey through this together in our coexistence.

With all of that being said, and with great excitement, we'd like to make this our official invitation for Indigenous people who see themselves in the work to speak about the show: moms, sisters, aunties, academics, community members, cuzzins, and friends, come hang out with us! We're having talkbacks and talking circles specifically for Indigenous Voices to be presenced and celebrated, so please check out the websites listed in this document for more details. We really would love to hear from the Indigenous community. DM us, grab us before or after the ceremony, tweet us, let's meet for tea, walks, and chats.

This story, this ceremony is for our Indigenous Peoples, it is to give voice and illuminate the power of Indigenous womxn. It is about our unwielded power and unsuppressed Settler supremacy for the entire journey of the artistic ceremony. That is the power we are reclaiming over our storytelling ceremony with *Kamloopa: An Indigenous Matriarch Story*.

With respect, in love and deep hope we can be vulnerable together to live courageously, we look forward to seeing you in the Long Lodge.

—Kim Senklip Harvey
　August 2018

Welcome to the *FIRE ZINE!* A Kamloopa *Study Buddy*

How are you feeling right now?
How are the people next to you feeling?
Take a moment to check in with yourself and the space you are in.

If you are with a group of people, here is an invitation to open a Talking Circle. This is a great way to connect with others, especially before entering the Indigenous artistic ceremony *Kamloopa*!

A simple offer is the question, "How are you feeling today?"

Step 1 - Begin by sitting in a circle with your group of people.

Step 2 - Designate an object to be your talking object - it can be anything at all (a pen, a rock, a sandwich)!

Step 3 - To begin, the person who is holding the talking object is the first and sole speaker, and they may share as little or as much as they like. This naturally creates space for everyone else to listen. Share in whatever way you'd like to, whether it be a long story or just a single word - whatever works!

Step 4 - After the speaker has shared, and when they are ready, they can pass the talking object on to the person next to them. Everyone gets an equal chance to share and check in, and also gets the opportunity to hold space for the other people in the circle. It is a good idea to just respond to the initial question (for example, "How are you doing?"). Let yourself take the time to share whatever you need to, and don't worry about responding to the person who has just finished speaking before you.

Step 5 - Once everyone has spoken, take a moment to let everything that has happened resonate.

 Congratulations! You just did a Talking Circle!

Indigenous Knowing Is Power!

What is Indigenous Knowing? Indigenous Knowing is an inherent understanding that is present and accessible within Indigenous Peoples. This knowledge can be passed down through generations and by Ancestors, too! Cool :). Knowledge can be revealed through dreams, received through intuition, can gradually present itself in a person over a period of time: there are many forms that knowledge may take, and all of these are valid, justifiable, respectable, powerful, and equally important ways of knowing! Indigenous Knowing exists in many times — it is connected to all elements of life and existence, and is completely in relation to physical and non-physical realms. Indigenous Knowing respects the spiritual and emotional life of all individuals — sources of knowledge are not placed within a hierarchical value system. As Indigenous Knowing is something that is inherently understood, it cannot always be explained and defined by a Western institutional standard. This Study Buddy would like to presence and underscore the beauty and importance of Indigenous Knowing, and highlight specifically the reclamation of Indigenous Knowing that is alive in Kamloopa! háy čxʷ qə!

New Definitions for Indigenous Theatre:
Fire Keepers

by Kim Senklip Harvey

Indigenous Matriarch Designation
[colonial theatre title]

Fire Creator
[playwright]

Fire Igniters
[playwright, directors, producers, dramaturges, designers, stage managers and assistant stage managers, administration]

Fire Tenders
[playwright, directors, producers, dramaturges, designers]

Fire Holders
[actors, stage-management team members, technicians, administration]

Fire Extinguishers
[actors, stage-management team members, technicians, administration]

movement

patterns

Wait! What Is Indigenous Theatre?

sphere

elemental

"And after being silenced for so long there was this overwhelming need to express ourselves with as few limitations as possible. The attitude was, 'Don't tell us what we can and can't do, just let us tell our stories in our own way. Let us see our culture reflected back to us in whatever fashion, and in whatever media we want.'"

—Carol Greyeyes, "On the Trail of Native Theatre"[2]

To offer any kind of concrete, simplified, or static answer to the question "What is Indigenous Theatre?" would not serve the readers of the *FIRE ZINE*. Instead, here are a few alternative offerings: The above quote from an essay by Carol Greyeyes, assistant professor and coordinator at the University of Sakatchewan's wîcêhtowin Theatre Program. The words from the Fire Keepers of *Kamloopa* on the same question, "What is Indigenous Theatre?", scattered gently around this page. As well, below are questions from "The Embodied Politics of Relational Indigenous Dramaturgies" by Fire Igniter / Tender / Dramaturge Dr. Lindsay Lachance[3] that you could bring to an Indigenous Theatre piece, or Indigenous artistic ceremony, in place of answers.

depth   *repeating*   *complexity*   *hair*

"When attending Indigenous Theatre, I might ask:

1. What biases or assumptions do I repeat without realizing?
2. What are the worldviews and tools that I carry with me and how can I utilize them in this situation?
3. How can I recognize and shift the gaze and the ears that I am using when attending theatre?
4. How can I develop the opportunity to listen, learn, and act in relationship to potential cultural differences?
5. How do I deal with refusals or cultural difference when I don't recognize or understand what I see onstage?
6. How can I be accountable to what I am experiencing and do the labour of self-educating when I don't fully understand the references being made?
7. For whose sake is the work being understood or categorized?"

FIRE ZINE! A Kamloopa *Study Buddy* would like to prioritize the idea of values in relation to *Kamloopa!*

why tho

Values are something that are intrinsic to a person – your values are what you feel are important in your life.

y not themes tho??

Values are specific to each individual, and we all have worthy, important, and different values from one another. Values are complete and nuanced, and yet remain permeable and changeable throughout your life - they are complex. They cannot be identified in a contained way, because they mean something different to every person.

K.

The Study Buddy would like to presence some of the values that are alive in *Kamloopa* in the following pages:
Indigenous Matriarchy
Time
Representation
Ceremony
and **Transformation**
(**Suggestion**: check out these pages after you witness the artistic ceremony *Kamloopa!*)

 VALUES SPECIAL INTRODUCTORY QUESTION:
What is your relationship to love?

Take in the word "matriarch." Really breathe it in, let it settle in your mind. What image arises? For many, the word might be associated with the image of an old, wizened, elderly woman, possibly smelling of soup. A beautiful image! HOWEVER! "Matriarch" could ALSO describe a younger woman in her twenties or thirties, much like Mikaya, Edith, and Kilawna: matriarchs can come in all ages and forms. Throughout the ceremony's journey, these women experience an ignition of their Indigenous Matriarchal power. Boom!

Indigenous Matriarchy can mean many, many things. For the Kamloopa team, Indigenous Matriarchy means:

//Resilience /Kinship /Resistance /Power /Generosity /Culture /Tenderness /Wisdom /Patience /Holding and Embracing /Space /Passing On /Raising /Warrior Women /Responsiveness /Understanding /Nimbleness /Intuition /Awareness /Equity /Acknowledgment /Loudness /Youth and Girls /Laughter /Reflection /Evolution /Intuition /Respect.

How has this play shifted your understanding of the word "matriarch"? What does "Indigenous Matriarchy" mean to you? Can you think of any matriarchs in your life that you would like to presence?

These words from the *Kamloopa Fire Keepers* offer an insight on what Indigenous relationality to time means:

Seasons, Songs, Impermanence, Stories, Rivers, The Cell, The Exchange, Static Moment, Memory, Moon Cycles, Water, Rising, Crashing, Tree Rings, Trickster, Layering, Change of Land.

Consider each word: What does each one mean to you according to your experience? What kind of images or memories appear? Do you have a different appreciation of a particular word than your neighbour's?

REPRESENTATION CORNER ➡

KAMLOOPA FEATURES MANY REFERENCES TO FILM AND TV FEATURING INDIGENOUS PEOPLES! THERE ARE ALSO REFERENCES TO MEDIA PORTRAYALS OF AN IDEA OR A PROJECTION OF AN INDIGENOUS PERSON WRITTEN AND PERFORMED BY NON-INDIGENOUS FOLKS.

BESIDES *KAMLOOPA*, CAN YOU THINK OF ANY EXAMPLES OF PORTRAYALS OF INDIGENOUS PEOPLES BY INDIGENOUS PEOPLES IN MEDIA THAT YOU HAVE WITNESSED RECENTLY?

Think back to Kim's Protocols for the Indigenous ceremony *Kamloopa*:
How were her words present for you during the play?

Kamloopa is a journey of protocols: it begins in the Longhouse with a
welcoming dance and ends with a hip-hop celebration! *Kamloopa*
challenges us to question our preconceived notions about protocol and
ceremony and the different forms they can exist in.

Here is an offering from the 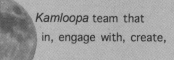 *Kamloopa* team that
shares ways they participate in, engage with, create,
and understand ceremony:

|Honour |Ritual |Medicine |Gather |WE KNOW
|Community |Family |Intention |Celebrate |Prayer
|Saved |Recovered |Conscious |Transcend |Shift
|New |Life |It Presents Itself |Intrinsic |Reclaimed|

What was your experience at the end of the play?
Did you have fun?!
How did you feel at the beginning?
Did you have any specific expectations for the
end of the play?

Transformation is a value present throughout *Kamloopa*: the transformation of the artistic ceremony space, of the experience of time, of bodies, and of relationships. Initially, in the play, Mikaya is having physical, emotional, spiritual, and intellectual experiences that are at first difficult to understand and feel. However, through the gradual recognition and ignition of her own power, Mikaya is able to transform and experience these feelings in a new way! Her transformation of how she experiences her inner power shifts her relationship to herself, her sisters, her Indigeneity, and her knowledge and strength.

Transformation Questions

What transformations in *Kamloopa* did you witness?
How does Mikaya transform her situation?
What tools does she find within herself?
What is *your* relationship to your own power?
What systems in your life aren't working for you?

Story Mode

Kamloopa is a story of friendship, support, love, and sisterhood. What makes *Kamloopa* different from a hero(ine)'s journey?
How do the elements of friendship, support, love, and sisterhood help ignite the power of Mikaya, Kilawna, and Edith?

......Wellness Corner

Welcome to the Wellness
Corner of the FIRE ZINE!

Above is a photo of the *Wellness Room* set up
by the Fire Keepers of Kamloopa in the backstage
area of the Western Canada Theatre in Kamloops
/ Tk'əmlúps, British Columbia. Its purpose was
to aid the Fire Keepers on their artistic journey.
Everyone needs a moment of wellness, especially
during a creative process! The process itself is
just as important as the performances. How do
you make yourself feel good?

<3 RESOURCES <3

Vancouver Aboriginal Friendship Centre
A non-profit organization that provides all kinds of resources for
Urban Indigenous people to help ignite the power within!
www.vafcs.org

Kamloops Aboriginal Friendship Society
A gorgeous website offering resources to Urban Indigenous people
from the Kamloops Aboriginal Friendship Society.
www.kafs.ca

Kanehsatake: 270 Years of Resistance
An amazing documentary by ~legendary~ Abenaki filmmaker
Alanis Obomsawin, filmed during the 1990 Kanien'kehá:ka land
dispute.
www.nfb.ca/film/kanehsatake_270_years_of_resistance/

Indigenous Foundations at UBC
A great resource provided by the University of British Columbia's
First Nations and Indigenous Studies program. The site features
key information on topics relating to and affecting the Indigenous
Peoples living in British Columbia – there is knowledge here for
everyone! Yay for learning!
indigenousfoundations.arts.ubc.ca/home/

Powwows Happening in British Columbia
Get yer dance on!
calendar.powwows.com/events/categories/pow-wows/pow-wows-in
-british-columbia/

Building the Fire podcast
A simply splendid podcast brought to you by the Fire Keepers of
Kamloopa!
anchor.fm/buildingthefire

Closing Circle

Phew!
Take a big ole breath:
you just received a lot of powerful info.
How was that for you?
We went so many places together. I invite you to partake in a
Closing Circle as a way to honour the work that you've just done.

Step 1 - Go back to the first pages of this zine to refresh
your Talking Circle facilitating power!

Step 2 - Pick a new Talking Object since we've
come so far - that sandwich probably
looks a little sketchy at this point...

Step 3 - Here are some potential, perfectly potent questions for your
Talking Circle:

How was the entire experience for you?
How do you feel now in comparison to how you felt at the Opening
Circle? Are there any changes?
What is a significant feeling or image that you have from *Kamloopa* or
the *FIRE ZINE*?

Step 4 - After everyone has spoken, take
a moment to let it all sink in.

Congratulations, and thank you for sharing!
We hope you are feeling an IGNITION OF POWER!
All the best vibes,
Study Buddy

Sources and Credits

The *Kamloopa* Fire Keeper Team is: Kim Senklip Harvey, with Cris Derksen, Yolanda Bonnell, Daniela Masellis, Lindsay Lachance, Jessica Schacht, Michelle Chabassol, Samantha Brown, Emily Soussana, Madison Henry, Kaitlyn Yott, and Samantha McCue.

FOOTNOTES

1. Lynn F. Lavallée, "Practical Application of an Indigenous Research Framework and Two Qualitative Indigenous Research Methods: Sharing Circles and Anishnaabe Symbol-Based Reflection," *International Journal of Qualitative Methods* 8, no. 1, 2005: 22, https://doi.org/10.1177/160940690900800103.

2. Carol Greyeyes, "On the Trail of Native Theatre," in *Performing Indigeneity*, ed. Yvette Nolan and Ric Knowles, New Essays on Canadian Theatre, vol. 6 (Toronto: Playwrights Canada Press, 2016), 99–100.

3. Lindsay Lachance, "The Embodied Politics of Relational Indigenous Dramaturgies" (Ph.D. diss., University of British Columbia, 2018), 12, https://dx.doi.org/10.14288/1.0363947.

OTHER SOURCES

Bartlett, Judith. "Health and Well-Being for Métis Women in Manitoba." *Canadian Journal of Public Health / Revue canadienne de santé publique* 96. Supplement 1, *Aboriginal Health Research and Policy: First Nations-University Collaboration in Manitoba* (January/February 2005): S22–S27. https://www.jstor.org/stable/41994445.

Harvey, Kim Senklip. "Protocols for the Indigenous Artistic Ceremony Kamloopa." Author's blog. August 20, 2018. https://www.kimsenklipharvey.com/single-post/2018/08/20/Protocols-for-the-Indigenous-Artistic-Ceremony-Kamloopa.

Iseke, Judy M. "Importance of Métis Ways of Knowing in Healing Communities." In "Connecting to Spirit in Indigenous Research." *Canadian Journal of Native Education* 33, no. 1 (2010).

Talking Together: A Discussion Guide for *Walking Together: First Nations, Métis and Inuit Perspectives in Curriculum*. "Talking Circle: Fact Sheet." Accessed August 2019. https://www.learnalberta.ca/content/aswt/talkingtogether/facilitated_talking_circle_fact_sheet.html.

* Background stock images sourced from unsplash.com. All other images used are intended for educational purposes only.

FIRE ZINE! A **Kamloopa** *Study Buddy* **ignited (with love) by Miki Wolf.**

ACKNOWLEDGMENTS TO:

the peoples of the xʷməθkʷəy̓əm, Sḵwx̱wú7mesh, Stó:lō, and səl̓ilwətaʔɬ Nations who generously allow me to be a guest on their Territories;

my Ancestors, for guiding me;

Mom, Dad, Kristen, and Karlene, I love you;

Aunties and Uncles and Cuzzzzins;

Gwen Benaway, Alicia Elliott, Quelemia Sparrow, Emilie LeClerc, Tai Amy Grauman, Miki Wolf;

Marie Clements, Margo Kane, Lisa Ravensbergen, Kevin Loring, Gordon Tootoosis;

Daryl Cloran, Lori Marchand, Heather Cant;

Brendon Lodge;

Pippa Mackie, Kevin Kerr;

Heather Redfern, Cindy Reid, Lisa Menille, Nicole McLuckie, Jennifer Dawn Bishop, James MacDonald, Dawn Bergstrom, Drove, Marcus Youssef, Mel Hague, Brian Quirt, Jenna Rodgers, and Daryl Ternowski;

the Tk'emlúps te Secwépemc Band, the Kamloopa Powwow, the Banff Cultural Leadership O.G. cohort, the Writing in a Racialized Canada cohort, National Theatre School of Canada / École nationale de théâtre du Canada, Sydney J. Risk and the Foundation, UBC's Department of Theatre and Film, the Jessie Richardson Theatre Awards, the Brookswood Secondary School's drama program, the Vancouver Murder men's roller derby team, the jury members who gave me money, the Honey Night at Mod Club, the Boston Pizza in Tk'emlúps / Kamloops, and Jamieson Vitamins;

Nancy Saddleman – translation Matriarch;

Charles Simard, my lovely editor, and the Talonbooks family.

So much gratitude and Indigenous love to you all ...

and Cheezies, for always being there for us.

The playwright also acknowledges the assistance of the 2018 Banff Playwrights Lab, a partnership between the Banff Centre for Arts and Creativity and the Canada Council for the Arts.

97

Kim Senklip Harvey is a proud Syilx, Tsilhqot'in, Ktunaxa, and Dakelh Nations womxn and is a Fire Creator (director / playwright / actor / community member) and Indigenous Cultural Evolutionist.

Past acting highlights include: *Rez Sisters, Ernestine Shuswap Gets Her Trout, The Laurier Memorial, Salmon Row*, the Governor General's Literary Award–winning play *Where the Blood Mixes*, the final show of Gordon Tootoosis's *Gordon Winter*, and the world premiere of *Children of God* at the National Arts Centre / Centre national des Arts.

In 2017, Kim participated in the residency Centering Ourselves: Writing in a Racialized Canada, which assembled twenty of Canada's most exciting PoC writers at the Banff Centre. She recently completed her two-year residency with the National Theatre School of Canada / École nationale de théâtre du Canada in their inaugural Artistic Leadership Residency program. Kim has been shortlisted for the Ontario Arts Foundation's Gina Wilkinson Prize for her work as a director and has participated in the Banff Playwrights Lab and the Rumble Theatre's Directors Lab.

In 2018, the play *Kamloopa: An Indigenous Matriarch Story* had a three-city world premiere. It won the 2019 Jessie Richardson Award for Significant Artistic Achievement – Outstanding Decolonizing Theatre Practices and Spaces, was the first Indigenous play in the Award's history to win Best Production, and was the 2019 recipient of the Sydney J. Risk Prize for Outstanding Original Play by an Emerging Playwright.

Kim is invested in community and youth engagement and has worked on the Mayor's Task Force on Mental Health and Addiction and the City of Vancouver's Urban Aboriginal Peoples' Advisory Committee. As Youth Program manager at The Cultch, she created, spearheaded, and fundraised the Indigenous Youth Initiative which focused on increasing the artistic opportunities of young urban Indigenous people in Metro Vancouver.

Kim's passion for theatre lives within its transformational nature. She believes that storytelling is the most compelling medium to move us to a place where every community member is provided the opportunity to live peacefully.